AF416406

Staying Scared - The Films of a Horror Movie Legend

Brian Dailey

Published by Indulge Media Group, 2023.

While every precaution has been taken in the preparation of this book, the publisher assumes no responsibility for errors or omissions, or for damages resulting from the use of the information contained herein.

STAYING SCARED - THE FILMS OF A HORROR MOVIE LEGEND

First edition. December 19, 2023.

Copyright © 2023 Brian Dailey.

ISBN: 979-8223642862

Written by Brian Dailey.

Table of Contents

Staying Scared - The Films of a Horror Movie Legend 1

Chapter 1: Night of the Living Dead: Birth of the Modern Zombie...7

Chapter 2: There's Always Vanilla: Romero's Departure from Horror 33

Chapter 3: Season of the Witch (Hungry Wives) 41

Chapter 7: The Crazies: Paranoia and Government Conspiracy 51

Chapter 4: The Amusement Park: See you at the park one day! 65

Chapter 6 - Martin: Exploring the Dark Side of Obsession 73

Chapter 7: Dawn of the Dead: Consumerism and Social Commentary 85

Chapter 8: Knightriders: Fighting the Dragon 99

Chapter 9: Creepshow: A Love Letter to Horror Anthologies 109

Chapter 10: Day of the Dead: The Last Stand of Humanity 129

Chapter 11: Monkey Shines: An Experiment in Fear 145

Chapter 12: Two Evil Eyes 161

Chapter 13: The Dark Half: Serious writer or serial killer. 173

Chapter 14: "Bruiser" Migration to Canada 181

Chapter 15: Land of the Dead: A World Divided by Class 189

Chapter 16:Diary of the Dead: Found Footage in the Zombie Genre 201

Chapter 17: Survival of the Dead: Exploring the Moral Dilemma .. 213

Chapter 18: The Legacy of George A. Romero: Impact on Horror Cinema...225

Dedicated to Jeanette

Erie, Pennsylvania, 1984. Wind howled through my attic bedroom, whispering secrets with the gnarled branches of the maple tree. Inside, I clutched a cardboard sleeve adorned with a skull-gnawing corpse under a moonlit sky. Across the room, Danielle, the girl who made my teenage heart stumble like a drunk ballerina, sat perched on the edge of my bed, a nervous flutter in her eyes. Tonight, we were about to trespass into the forbidden territory of George A. Romero's Night of the Living Dead, courtesy of the Home Video Exchange on Peach Street – a dimly lit emporium of sketchy VHS tapes and whispered rumors.

This wasn't your squeaky-clean Blockbuster. The proprietor sported a permanent five-o'clock shadow and a knowing smirk etched from leather. He handed me the tape, his gravelly voice echoing in the fluorescent haze, "Scary flick, huh, kid?" I gulped, feeling the heat creep up my neck, and retreated into the Erie night, clutching the box like a holy grail.

Back in my attic, we settled in. The opening credits crawled across the screen, discordant moans leaching from the flickering television. Then, boom! Johnny's head met the tombstone in a symphony of crunching bone. Danielle, who moments ago was munching popcorn with the nonchalance of a seasoned horror veteran, froze. The color drained from her face, replaced by a sickly green that rivaled the moss clinging to Jordy Verrill in Creepshow. The popcorn turned a forgotten casualty in her lap, and before the next scene could even unfold, she unleashed a series of retches that would make Linda Blair proud.

Heroically, I paused the tape (VHS technology, remember?) and became the knight in shining tissues, battling both nausea and the ghosts of a poorly-timed hot dog. Tears welled up in Danielle's eyes, and soon, a minivan pulled up like a rescue chariot, her sniffling sobs dissolving into the night.

Alone again, the silence felt different. Fear, that elusive beast, hadn't materialized. Instead, a spark of morbid fascination crackled in its place. I hit play, and as Johnny's vacant eyes stared back from the screen, I knew something had shifted. This wasn't just a bad date gone wrong; it was a baptism into a new cinematic religion. The grainy black and white, the clunky pacing, the relentless dread – it was unlike anything I'd ever seen, and I was irrevocably hooked.

This book is a love letter to the man who redefined horror, George A. Romero. It's a pilgrimage through the graveyard of his celluloid creations, from the bleak landscapes of Night of the Living Dead to the neon-drenched malls of Dawn of the Dead, from the claustrophobic bunkers of Day of the Dead to the desolate highways of Land of the Dead. It's an excavation of Romero's social commentary, a celebration of his gore-soaked artistry, and a testament to his power to linger long after the credits roll.

Some call him the Godfather of the Zombie. Others, a master of macabre. To me, he's simply George – a storyteller who spun nightmares from the threads of our anxieties, a filmmaker who dared to hold a mirror up to our darkest reflections. This book is my attempt to polish that mirror, to clear away the dust and scratches, and show you the audacity, and the sheer unsettling brilliance of his work.

So, whether you're a seasoned cinephile or a curious newcomer, crack open this book like a VHS tape and step into the world of George Romero. Prepare to be scared, to be challenged, to be entertained. Just remember, if you do get a little green...well, blame Johnny. But mostly, blame George. Because trust me, his films have a way of staying with you, lingering in the corners of your mind like the shadows of a maple tree at midnight. -Brian

Welcome to "Staying Scared - The Films of a Horror Movie Legend." In this book, we delve into the captivating world of one of horror cinema's most iconic directors, George A. Romero. Known for his groundbreaking work in the zombie genre, Romero's films have left an indelible mark on the history of horror. From his debut feature "Night of the Living Dead" to his later works like "Land of the Dead" and "Diary of the Dead," Romero's films continue to terrify and entertain audiences.

In the heart of the Bronx, New York City, on a cold winter's day, February 4, 1940, a legend was born. George Andrew Romero, a child of Anne Romero (Dvorsky) and George Romero, a commercial artist, was destined to leave an indelible mark on the world of cinema.

Romero's childhood was steeped in the magic of film. He would often journey into the heart of Manhattan, returning with reels of film that he would watch in the comfort of his home. One film that captured his imagination was the opera-based "The Tales of Hoffmann", a fascination he shared with another future director, Martin Scorsese.

Romero's love for film led him to the hallowed halls of Carnegie Mellon University in Pittsburgh. Here, he immersed himself in the study of art and design, laying the groundwork for his illustrious career in filmmaking. Upon leaving school, he delivered newsreels to local stations in Pittsburgh. He dabbled in commercial art and directed television commercials, one of which was a segment for Mister Rogers' Neighborhood.

In the late 1960s, Romero and nine friends, including screenwriter John A. Russo, formed Image Ten Productions. This venture would give birth to "Night of the Living Dead" (1968), a film that would become a cult classic and redefine modern horror cinema. This film marked the beginning of Romero's "Night of the Living Dead" series, which painted a chilling picture of a zombie apocalypse and shaped the image of the zombie in modern culture.

Romero's early life was filled with passion for film and storytelling. His experiences in New York and Pittsburgh, his Lithuanian and Spanish-Cuban heritage, and his education at Carnegie Mellon University all played a role in shaping him into the influential filmmaker he would become. His early works, particularly "Night of the Living Dead", would forever change the landscape of the horror film genre and cement his legacy as the "Father of the Zombie Film".

Romero's films are known for their social commentary and exploration of deeper themes within the horror genre. His zombie films, in particular, served as a reflection of societal issues such as consumerism, government control, and class divide. Through his unique storytelling and innovative filmmaking techniques, Romero became a pioneer in the genre, influencing countless filmmakers and leaving a lasting legacy.

In the following chapters, we will explore each of Romero's films in detail, analyzing their themes, impact, and cultural significance. From the birth of the modern zombie in "Night of the Living Dead" to the moral dilemmas of "Survival of the Dead," each chapter will provide a comprehensive look into the world of George A. Romero's films.

So, grab your popcorn and get ready to dive into the world of George A. Romero. Whether you're a die-hard fan or new to his work, "Staying Scared - The Films of a Horror Movie Legend" is sure to satisfy your craving for all things horror.

Chapter 1: Night of the Living Dead: Birth of the Modern Zombie

In this chapter, we will explore George A. Romero's groundbreaking film, "Night of the Living Dead," which is widely regarded as the birth of the modern zombie genre. Released in 1968, this low-budget independent film not only terrified audiences but also challenged societal norms and paved the way for a new era of horror cinema.

"Night of the Living Dead" follows a group of strangers who find themselves trapped in a farmhouse while hordes of reanimated corpses, commonly referred to as zombies, roam the countryside, craving human flesh. As the survivors fight to stay alive, tensions rise, and the film delves into themes of fear, racism, and the breakdown of social order.

This film was revolutionary for its time, as it introduced the concept of flesh-eating zombies and portrayed them in a more realistic and terrifying manner. Romero's zombies were not the slow-moving creatures we often associate with the genre today but rather relentless, flesh-hungry monsters that created a sense of urgency and danger for the characters.

The impact of "Night of the Living Dead" cannot be overstated. It challenged the conventions of horror filmmaking, defying expectations and pushing boundaries. At a time when the horror genre was dominated by supernatural creatures like vampires and werewolves, Romero's film brought horror into the realm of everyday life. The zombies in "Night of the Living Dead" were not products of the supernatural but rather the result of a mysterious radiation-induced phenomenon, making them all the more terrifying.

Social Commentary

One of the most significant aspects of "Night of the Living Dead" is its social commentary. The film was released in a time of social upheaval, with the Civil Rights Movement and the Vietnam War dominating the cultural landscape. Romero used the zombie apocalypse as a metaphor for the chaos and fear that gripped society during this time period.

The character of Ben, played by Duane Jones, is a black man who becomes the de facto leader of the group. This was a bold and progressive choice for the time, as it challenged racial stereotypes and addressed issues of racism in America. The film's shocking and tragic ending, in which Ben is mistaken for a zombie and shot by a group of white vigilantes, further highlights these themes and leaves a lasting impact on the audience.

"Night of the Living Dead" - a name that sends chills down the spine of horror movie enthusiasts. The film owes its success to the talented cast who breathed life into the characters. Let's delve into the lives of these remarkable individuals.

Before "Night of the Living Dead," Hollywood clung to tired tropes that relegated Black actors to subservient or comedic roles. Jones, however, defied convention. Ben, the film's protagonist, is not a sidekick or a victim. He is a complex, resourceful leader, thrust into a nightmarish reality. He acts with decisiveness, protecting Barbra and the other survivors, even as the world crumbles around them. Jones imbues Ben with a quiet dignity, his every action laced with a pragmatic understanding of the horrors they face. He is not a superhero, but an ordinary man forced into extraordinary circumstances, making him all the more relatable and heroic.

The casting of Jones, a Black man, in this leading role was revolutionary. Prior to "Night of the Living Dead," Black actors rarely found themselves at the forefront of the story, let alone in horror films. Jones's presence challenged deeply ingrained racial biases, forcing audiences to confront their own preconceptions. Ben's intelligence, his courage, and his humanity stand in stark contrast to the mindless, flesh-eating zombies surrounding him. He becomes a symbol of resilience in the face of overwhelming odds, a reflection of the struggles for social justice and equality that were roiling American society at the time.

The cultural impact of Jones's portrayal of Ben extends far beyond the initial shock of his casting. He rewrote the rules of how Black characters could be depicted on screen. Ben is not defined by his race, but by his actions and his choices. He is flawed, capable of violence and anger, yet ultimately driven by a desire to protect himself and others. This complexity humanized the Black male figure in a way rarely seen before, offering a much-needed corrective to harmful stereotypes.

Jones's contribution to cinematic history goes beyond representation. His nuanced performance elevates the film to a level of social commentary rarely seen in the horror genre. "Night of the Living Dead" isn't just about zombies; it's about the breakdown of society, the fragility of human life, and the inherent racism that fuels both fear and violence. Jones's presence underscores these themes, his every move a challenge to the status quo, a poignant indictment of a society failing to confront its own inner demons.

The ending of "Night of the Living Dead" is tragically poetic. Ben, mistaken for a zombie by a panicked mob, is gunned down. This brutal moment underscores the film's central message: we often fear what we don't understand, and that fear can have deadly consequences. It is also a stark reminder of the real-world dangers faced by Black communities, where prejudice and discrimination can lead to fatal encounters.

While "Night of the Living Dead" remains Jones's defining performance, his career offers a testament to his versatility. He appeared in films like "Ganja & Hess," a groundbreaking Blaxploitation film, and "Gladiator," a science fiction thriller. He even took the helm as director, showcasing his multifaceted talents both on and off-screen.

Duane Jones's legacy is not confined to the silver screen. He was a vocal advocate for civil rights and used his platform to champion social justice causes. He understood the power of film to challenge societal norms and inspire change, and he wielded that power with grace and purpose.

In conclusion, Duane Jones's contributions to cinema extend far beyond mere acting. He broke down racial barriers, redefined the cinematic hero, and used his platform to address critical social issues. Jones's legacy is a reminder that film can be more than just entertainment; it can be a powerful tool for social change, and through his groundbreaking work, he ensured that future generations of actors and audiences would never see the world, or cinema, in the same way again.

Judith O'Dea, a Pittsburgh native with aspirations of becoming a filmmaker, stumbled upon the "Night of the Living Dead" audition by chance. Thrust into the role with minimal preparation, she brought a vulnerability and immediacy to Barbra that resonated deeply with audiences. Barbra is not the typical damsel in distress. She is terrified, yes, but also fiercely determined to survive, navigating the post-apocalyptic wasteland with a raw courage that transcends genre conventions.

O'Dea's performance defied expectations on multiple fronts. In a time when Hollywood rarely cast women in leading roles, let alone women in horror, Barbra is the undeniable protagonist. She makes choices, drives the narrative, and grapples with the moral complexities of the situation. More importantly, O'Dea's portrayal shattered racial barriers. In 1968, a Black protagonist in a horror film was practically unheard of. Yet, Barbra's race is never explicitly addressed, making her universality all the more powerful.

Beyond her on-screen presence, O'Dea's impact extends to the film's production itself. With a shoestring budget and a fledgling crew, "Night of the Living Dead" relied heavily on improvisation and resourcefulness. O'Dea actively contributed to the creative process, collaborating with Romero and the other actors to flesh out the characters and the story. This collaborative spirit added a layer of authenticity that resonated with viewers and cemented the film's cult status.

"Night of the Living Dead" wasn't just a horror movie; it was a social commentary disguised as a zombie flick. O'Dea understood this subtext and imbued Barbra with a quiet desperation that mirrored the anxieties of a society grappling with racial tensions, the Vietnam War, and a growing distrust of authority. Barbra's journey wasn't just about survival; it was a metaphor for the struggles for social justice and the search for meaning in a seemingly chaotic world.

O'Dea's career extended beyond "Night of the Living Dead," though Barbra's shadow inevitably loomed large. She appeared in various television shows and independent films, even returning to the role of Barbra in the 2017 sequel "Night of the Living Dead: Genesis." However, it is her first foray into the undead that continues to define her legacy.

Today, Judith O'Dea remains a beloved figure in the horror community, actively engaging with fans and advocating for independent film. Her impact is undeniable. She helped dismantle harmful stereotypes, redefined the female hero in horror, and lent her voice to a film that became a cultural touchstone. "Night of the Living Dead" may be a product of its time, but O'Dea's portrayal of Barbra transcends those boundaries, offering a timeless scream that continues to echo through the corridors of cinema.

O'Dea's contribution to horror goes far beyond a single iconic performance. She defied expectations, challenged norms, and breathed life into a character who became a symbol of resilience and survival. Barbra's scream may have been born in a Pennsylvania cemetery, but it reverberated around the world, forever altering the landscape of horror and cementing O'Dea's place as a true legend of the genre.

While the names Judith O'Dea and Duane Jones instantly conjure up images of flesh-eating ghouls and groundbreaking social commentary in the minds of horror fans, the impact of "Night of the Living Dead" wouldn't be the same without the multifaceted contributions of the late Karl Hardman. Although best known for his portrayal of the domineering patriarch Harry Cooper, Hardman's involvement in the film stretched far beyond a single role, making him a vital yet often overlooked thread in the tapestry of this horror masterpiece.

Born in Pittsburgh in 1927, Hardman's artistic journey began in radio before transitioning to television in the 1950s. He established himself as a versatile performer, showcasing his comedic chops and later venturing into dramatic territory with his own production company. It was through that Hardman crossed paths with Romero, a young filmmaker with a revolutionary vision for a low-budget zombie flick.

Hardman's initial involvement with "Night of the Living Dead" was primarily logistical. He helped secure funding, recruited talent, and even handled the film's sound effects. But when the actor originally cast as Harry Cooper dropped out, Hardman, ever the versatile artist, stepped in.

Hardman's portrayal of Harry is a masterclass in nuanced villainy. Gone are the over-the-top theatrics often associated with horror villains. Instead, Hardman delivers a chillingly relatable performance, a man driven by a distorted sense of family loyalty and the desperate need to maintain control in the face of utter chaos. His final confrontation with Ben, a desperate struggle for power fueled by fear and misunderstanding, is a tour de force of character acting that stays with you long after the credits roll.

But Hardman's contributions to "Night of the Living Dead" extend far beyond his on-screen presence. He served as a mentor to the young Romero, offering guidance and support throughout the grueling production process. He even applied the makeup to many of the film's ghouls, lending his artistic touch to the iconic look of the living dead.

The success of "Night of the Living Dead" catapulted Hardman into unexpected fame, forever tying him to the legacy of the zombie genre. Hardman passed away in 2007, leaving behind a rich legacy that extends far beyond the single role he is often remembered for. He was a versatile performer, a resourceful producer, a dedicated mentor, and a vital part of the team that brought the nightmare of "Night of the Living Dead" to life. He was, in the truest sense, a man of many faces, each facet adding depth and complexity to the story of a film that continues to terrify and inspire generations of viewers.

He wasn't just an actor; he was a builder, a mentor, and a vital cog in the engine that brought Romero's vision to life. While his gruff portrayal of Harry Cooper may be his most recognizable role, his behind-the-scenes contributions and commitment to the project ensure that his legacy extends far beyond the silver screen. He is a reminder that the success of any great film is rarely the result of a single individual, but rather a tapestry woven from the talents and dedication of many. And in the twisted, terrifying tapestry of "Night of the Living Dead," Karl Hardman's threads shine bright, a testament to the many faces of fear and the collaborative spirit that brought them to life.

In the graveyard of classic horror films, where heroes rise and fall and zombies groan with insatiable hunger, one name often goes unrecognized: Marilyn Eastman. While her onscreen portrayal of Helen Cooper in George A. Romero's 1968 masterpiece "Night of the Living Dead" remains poignant and chilling, Eastman's contributions to the film extend far beyond a single role. She was a multifaceted artist, a financial supporter, and a quiet force behind the scenes, forever leaving her mark on cinema history.

Eastman, born in Pittsburgh in 1933, was no stranger to the stage and screen. A seasoned actress and singer, she had years of experience in theater and radio before "Night of the Living Dead" came knocking. When Romero presented his low-budget zombie vision, Eastman saw not just a film, but a chance to challenge audiences and make a statement.

But her involvement went beyond acting. With the film's budget precariously thin, Eastman stepped up as a financial investor, using her own resources to help bring the project to life. This crucial support allowed Romero and his team to push the boundaries of independent filmmaking and create a horror experience that would resonate for generations.

On screen, Eastman embodied Helen Cooper, a mother caught in the throes of unimaginable horror. Her performance is a masterclass in emotional vulnerability and raw desperation. As she confronts the loss of her daughter turned zombie, grapples with the crumbling world around her, and navigates the conflicting personalities of the other survivors, Eastman delivers a performance that is both heartbreaking and hauntingly human.

Though Helen's fate is ultimately tragic, Eastman's contributions to "Night of the Living Dead" extend beyond her acting. She also contributed to the film's editing, makeup, and even props. This dedication to the project as a whole reflects her deep understanding of storytelling and her unwavering commitment to Romero's vision.

While Eastman continued to act in various films and television shows throughout her career, her role as Helen Cooper remains her most iconic.

Keith Wayne, a stage name borne by Ronald Keith Hartman, stands as a fascinating footnote in horror history. His sole on screen credit, the role of Tom in George A. Romero's groundbreaking 1968 masterpiece "Night of the Living Dead," remains forever etched in the nightmares of cinephiles. While Wayne's career beyond that iconic performance was brief and multifaceted, his impact on the film and its cultural implications deserves a closer look.

Born in Washington, Pennsylvania, in 1945, Wayne initially pursued a career in music, showcasing his talents as a singer, dancer, and musician. It was through these artistic pursuits that he crossed paths with the fledgling filmmaker George A. Romero. When Romero presented his idea for a low-budget zombie flick, Wayne, attracted by the project's novelty and social commentary, was among the first to sign on.

On screen, Wayne embodies Tom, a level-headed and resourceful individual thrust into the chaos of the living dead apocalypse. He becomes a leader amongst the survivors, his practical approach and quick thinking offering a stark contrast to the panicked hysteria surrounding them. While Wayne's acting might not be as nuanced as some of his co-stars, he delivers a believable and grounded performance, anchoring the film with a sense of normalcy amidst the surreal horror.

While the chilling screams and flesh-hungry ghouls of "Night of the Living Dead" (1968) often steal the spotlight, the quiet resilience of Judith Ridley's Judy stands as a beacon of hope in the film's bleak landscape. Her performance, grounded and relatable, offers a poignant counterpoint to the chaos and fear, reminding us of the strength and resourcefulness that lies within even the most unprepared individuals.

Ridley, born in Pittsburgh in 1946, stumbled upon "Night of the Living Dead" through a friend's connection to the production. Despite having no prior acting experience, her natural instincts and genuine emotional range caught the attention of director George A. Romero, who offered her the role of Judy, a young woman seeking refuge in the farmhouse alongside the other survivors.

Unlike the archetypal damsel in distress often found in horror films, Judy embodies a sense of self-preservation and practicality. She's quick to understand the gravity of the situation, offering emotional support to the traumatized Barbra while contributing to the group's survival efforts. Ridley's subtle, nuanced performance brings depth to Judy, portraying her not as a helpless victim but as a woman determined to overcome the horrors surrounding her.

Beyond her onscreen presence, Ridley played a vital role in the film's production. Her lack of previous acting experience made her a blank slate, allowing Romero to tailor Judy's character to fit Ridley's natural strengths and instincts. This collaborative approach resulted in a portrayal that feels fresh and genuine, adding a layer of authenticity to the film's already groundbreaking realism.

He shuffled onto the screen in 1968, a lumbering figure with vacant eyes and a hunger for flesh. He didn't speak, he didn't explain himself, he simply existed – a decaying embodiment of horror, a primal manifestation of humanity's darkest fears. This was S. William Hinzman's "Cemetery Zombie," the first flesh-eating ghoul in George A. Romero's groundbreaking "Night of the Living Dead," and a character whose impact on the horror genre and beyond remains significant even decades later.

Hinzman, born in Pennsylvania in 1936, wasn't a seasoned actor when he stumbled upon "Night of the Living Dead". A cinematographer and makeup artist by trade, his connection to the film came through his friendship with John Russo, Romero's co-writer. Recognizing Hinzman's imposing stature and quiet menace, Romero offered him the pivotal role of the first zombie viewers would encounter.

What followed was a performance that defied conventions. Unlike the slow-moving, mindless shamblers we associate with contemporary zombie lore, Hinzman's creation possessed an unsettling energy. He moved quicker, he chased, he clawed, fueled by a raw, primal hunger that defied the traditional depiction of zombies as slow, moaning masses. His makeup, simple yet effective, emphasized the character's decomposing flesh and bloodshot eyes, adding a visceral layer of realism to the portrayal.

Hinzman's impact extends far beyond his onscreen presence. He played a crucial role in the film's production, offering his makeup expertise to create the ghoulish visages of the other zombies. He even helped with sound effects, ensuring the guttural groans and unsettling moans resonated with audiences long after the credits rolled.

More importantly, Hinzman's "Cemetery Zombie" set the template for the modern zombie. He established the core attributes we have come to associate with these undead creatures – the insatiable hunger, the relentless pursuit, the lack of remorse or humanity. His performance challenged the boundaries of horror, introducing a visceral fear of reanimated corpses that transcended the limitations of the screen.

The significance of Hinzman's contribution goes beyond the genre itself. "Night of the Living Dead" was a film steeped in social commentary, using the zombie apocalypse as a metaphor for societal anxieties about race, war, and the breakdown of authority. Hinzman's zombie, with its atavistic hunger and mindless aggression, embodied these anxieties, serving as a stark reminder of the darkness that lurks beneath the surface of human civilization.

His legacy continues to inspire. Countless zombie films and television shows have drawn inspiration from Hinzman's groundbreaking performance, from the fast-paced runners of "28 Days Later" to the decaying hordes of "The Walking Dead." He has become a pop culture icon, his image instantly recognizable, his influence omnipresent in the modern landscape of horror.

Tragically, Hinzman passed away in 2012, leaving behind a legacy that far outlives his earthly presence. Though his career never took him beyond the realm of independent horror, his role in "Night of the Living Dead" cemented his place in cinematic history. He wasn't just an actor; he was a pioneer, a man who helped redefine a genre and unleashed a new breed of monster onto the world.

Finally, Kyra Schon, who played Karen Cooper, is the daughter of Karl Hardman.

Imagine the childhood spent on a horror film set, your dad the legendary Karl Hardman. That's Kyra Schon's reality, though she left the screams and trowels behind to forge a path of vibrant creativity. Today, she crafts intricate jewelry, paints playful pups, and even dispenses wisdom to both the living and the undead with her column. Kyra's story is a testament to the transformative power of art, a reminder that even the darkest beginnings can bloom into something beautiful.

Cinematic Techniques

Despite its low budget, "Night of the Living Dead" showcased Romero's skill as a filmmaker. The black-and-white cinematography added to the film's gritty and realistic atmosphere, while the use of handheld cameras and documentary-style filmmaking techniques enhanced the sense of immediacy and chaos. These techniques, combined with the film's intense and claustrophobic setting, created a sense of unease and tension that kept audiences on the edge of their seats.

Here are some quick facts about the 1968 film "Night of the Living Dead" by George A. Romero:

- The original idea for the film was an alien comedy.

- The film was made on a budget of just $114,000.

- It was shot in black and white in Pittsburgh.

- Duane Jones, who played Ben, rewrote some of his character's dialogue.

- The film is considered to have spawned the zombie genre.

- Despite its success, Romero saw very little profit from the film.

- The film grossed approximately $30 million, over 263 times its budget.

- At the time of its release, the film generated controversy due to its gore and macabre content.

"Night of the Living Dead" was a critical success, earning widespread acclaim and solidifying Romero's status as a master of horror. The film's impact can still be felt in the zombie genre today, with countless films, TV shows, and video games drawing inspiration from Romero's vision.

Romero's use of zombies as a metaphor for societal issues has also become a staple of the genre. His films challenged audiences to confront their own fears and prejudices while providing thrilling and thought-provoking entertainment.

The film is often credited as the origin of the modern zombie genre. Although the term "zombie" was never used in the film, the undead creatures in the movie, referred to as "ghouls," follow certain rules that have since become standard in zombie films.

- The first rule established in "Night of the Living Dead" is the concept of reanimation. The undead in the film are reanimated corpses, brought back to life by unknown means. This rule has become a staple in the zombie genre, with most films and series featuring zombies as reanimated corpses

- Another rule introduced in "Night of the Living Dead" is the zombies' insatiable craving for human flesh. This rule has also become a standard in the genre, with zombies often depicted as mindless creatures driven by their hunger for human flesh.

- In "Night of the Living Dead," the zombies come in greater numbers as the night goes by, and they use nasty tactics. This rule adds a sense of urgency and danger to the film, as the characters must constantly be on guard against the increasing number of zombies.

- The film also establishes that defenses against zombies can be unreliable. The characters in the film barricade themselves in a house, but the barricades may fall at any time. This rule adds an element of suspense to the film, as the characters can never truly feel safe.

"Night of the Living Dead" established several rules regarding zombies that have since become standard in the genre. These rules have not only shaped the way zombies are portrayed in films and series but have also influenced games and other forms of media. The impact of these rules is a testament to the enduring influence of "Night of the Living Dead" on the zombie genre.

A Fatal Oversight. The tragedy began with a seemingly innocuous error. The film's distributor, the Walter Reade Organization, failed to include a copyright notice on the prints. This oversight occurred during the transition from the film's original title, "Night of the Flesh Eaters", to its final title, "Night of the Living Dead".

In 1968, the absence of a copyright notice was not a trivial matter. According to the copyright laws of the time, a work would automatically enter the public domain if it lacked a proper notice. Thus, the moment "Night of the Living Dead" was screened, it was, in effect, everyone's property.

The Unseen Consequences

The repercussions of this error were far-reaching. The film, now in the public domain, could be freely distributed and viewed. This led to a flood of unauthorized home video releases, each one depriving Romero and his team of their well-deserved royalties. The film grossed over $30 million at the box office, a staggering sum for the late 1960s. Yet, Romero saw only a fraction of this wealth.

The home video market, which could have been a significant source of income, was similarly out of reach. Numerous companies released copies of "Night of the Living Dead", all without needing to pay a single cent to its creators. Romero's masterpiece was freely available to all, and yet, its creators were left empty-handed.

Despite the financial loss, "Night of the Living Dead" remains a seminal work in the horror genre. Its influence is evident in the countless zombie movies and TV shows that have since become a staple of popular culture. Romero's creative vision and independent spirit continue to inspire filmmakers around the world.

In the vast landscape of horror cinema, few films have achieved the enduring legacy and cultural significance of "Night of the Living Dead" (1968). Released over five decades ago, George A. Romero's low-budget masterpiece continues to captivate audiences and spawn countless imitations and adaptations. What is it about this black-and-white zombie film that continues to resonate with viewers? Let us explore the possible reasons why folks still connect with "Night of the Living Dead."

First and foremost, "Night of the Living Dead" broke new ground in the horror genre. It revolutionized the concept of the zombie, transforming them from voodoo-controlled slaves to flesh-eating ghouls. Romero's vision introduced the notion of the undead feasting on human flesh, an idea that would become a staple in subsequent zombie films. The film's shocking violence and graphic depictions of gore challenged the boundaries of what was considered acceptable on-screen, leaving a lasting impact on both horror and cinema as a whole.

"Night of the Living Dead" tapped into deep-seated fears and anxieties prevalent in society during the late 1960s. Released amidst the backdrop of the civil rights movement and the Vietnam War, the film subtly explored themes of racial tensions and social upheaval. The casting of African-American actor Duane Jones as the lead protagonist, Ben, was groundbreaking for its time. Ben's struggle for survival in the face of both the undead and human prejudice gave the film a powerful social commentary that resonated with audiences then and now.

Another reason for the film's enduring appeal lies in its raw and gritty atmosphere. Shot in black and white on a shoestring budget, "Night of the Living Dead" exudes a sense of realism and authenticity. The grainy visuals and stark cinematography add to the film's sense of unease and claustrophobia. The use of real locations, such as an actual farmhouse, further enhances the film's believability, making the audience feel as though they are experiencing the horror firsthand.

The characters in "Night of the Living Dead" are relatable and multidimensional, adding depth to the story. Despite their dire circumstances, the film explores the complexities of human nature and the dynamics that emerge when people are pushed to their limits. The conflicts and tensions among the survivors trapped in the farmhouse create a palpable sense of suspense and drama, keeping viewers on the edge of their seats.

The film's shocking and unforgettable climax is yet another reason why it continues to leave a lasting impression. The nihilistic ending, with Ben's tragic fate, subverted audience expectations and challenged the notion of a traditional Hollywood hero. This bold narrative choice left viewers unsettled and provoked discussions about the nature of horror and the human condition.

"Night of the Living Dead" possesses a timeless quality that transcends its era. Its themes of survival, fear, and the fragility of society are universal and resonate with audiences across generations. The film's influence can be seen in the countless zombie films, TV shows, and video games that have followed in its footsteps, cementing its status as a true classic.

Its groundbreaking approach to horror, social commentary, gritty atmosphere, relatable characters, shocking climax, and timeless themes have solidified its position as a cinematic masterpiece. As long as there are audiences seeking thrills, chills, and profound reflections on the human condition, "Night of the Living Dead" will continue to hold a special place in the annals of horror cinema.

Night of the Living Dead gets restored.

The original camera negative, a treasure carefully guarded by the members of Image Ten, the Pittsburgh partnership that originally produced the film, served as the foundation for this ambitious project. Under the watchful eyes of Romero himself and key members of Image Ten, including Gary Streiner, Russ Streiner, and John Russo, the restoration process began.

The task was entrusted to the skilled hands at Cineric Inc, NYC, and Audio Mechanics, Burbank, CA. Their mission was to create a 4K digital restoration that would do justice to the film's original brilliance. The project was generously funded by the George Lucas Family Foundation and the Celeste Bartos Fund for Film Preservation.

Cineric Inc., a leading film restoration company, was entrusted with the visual restoration. They meticulously scanned the original camera negative frame by frame using a 4K scanner, enhancing the visual quality while preserving the original monochrome aesthetic.

Meanwhile, Audio Mechanics was responsible for the audio restoration. They painstakingly enhanced the film's original sound, ensuring that the suspenseful moments were as impactful as in the original release.

The restored version premiered at New York's Film Forum in October 2017 to rave reviews. This project not only breathed new life into a classic film but also set a benchmark for future restoration projects.

The result was nothing short of spectacular. The restored version of "Night of the Living Dead" made its grand debut at MoMA as part of the Open Door Fridays series. It was also showcased in the To Save and Project Festival, a celebration of newly preserved and restored films.

But this restoration did more than just enhance the film's visual quality. It underscored the film's cultural impact, from its groundbreaking casting of an African American leading man, Duane Jones, to its innovative use of the zombie as a metaphorical figure. This film, reborn, continues to leave an indelible mark on our culture, and in my own life personally.

Chapter 2: There's Always Vanilla: Romero's Departure from Horror

George A. Romero is primarily known for his contributions to the horror genre, particularly his iconic zombie films. However, there was a time in his career when he decided to venture outside the realm of horror and experiment with different genres.

One such departure from the horror genre was the film "There's Always Vanilla" (1971).

A Shift in Genre

Released in 1971, "There's Always Vanilla" marked Romero's foray into romantic comedy. The film tells the story of Chris Bradley, a young man who returns home from the Army and struggles to find his place in society. He becomes involved with a young woman named Lynn, and their relationship unfolds against the backdrop of social and political unrest.

Romero's Exploration of Societal Issues

While "There's Always Vanilla" may not have achieved the same level of recognition as Romero's horror films, it is an important piece in his filmography. The movie explores themes of generational conflict, societal disillusionment, and the impact of war on individuals. Romero uses the romantic comedy genre as a platform to comment on the turbulent times of the late 1960s and early 1970s.

"There's Always Vanilla" - a film that marked a milestone in the careers of its cast. Let's take a closer look at these talented individuals.

Raymond Laine, a luminary in the realm of film, was born on April 9, 1936, in Pittsburgh, Pennsylvania, USA. His illustrious career spanned acting and writing, leaving an indelible mark on the industry. His contributions to the film world were not confined to acting. Laine also showcased his creative prowess as a writer, contributing additional material for "The Devil and Sam Silverstein" (1976).

Beyond the silver screen, Laine's influence permeated the theatrical world. He was a stalwart at Pittsburgh's Playhouse of Point Park College, acting professionally for over two decades. His roles as a director and acting coach at the college allowed him to shape the careers of many aspiring actors.

In essence, Raymond Laine was a multifaceted talent whose contributions to the film world were profound. His performances, particularly in "There's Always Vanilla," were memorable. His creative abilities shone through his writing, and his influence on the next generation of actors was significant. Despite his passing on November 1, 2000, in Pittsburgh, Pennsylvania, USA, his legacy continues to inspire and influence the film industry. His story is a testament to the enduring power of talent and creativity.

Born on September 15, 1946, in Pittsburgh, Pennsylvania, USA, Judith Ridley is a remarkable actress who has left an indelible mark on the film industry. Her performance in the 1971 romantic comedy "There's Always Vanilla," where she played the character of Lynn Harris was spectacular. The film traces the journey of Chris Bradley, a former U.S. Army soldier turned drifter, who meets Lynn at a local train station. Ridley's portrayal of Lynn, an older woman who becomes the emotional and financial anchor for Chris, added a layer of depth and complexity to the film.

Ridley's contributions to the film world extended beyond acting. She served as a receptionist for Karl Hardman and Marilyn Eastman's company, and later for George A. Romero's company, The Latent Image. She also worked as a food dresser for commercials, arranging and designing food to look as appealing as possible.

Here are some intriguing facts about the 1971 film "There's Always Vanilla" by George A. Romero:

- George A. Romero himself referred to it as his worst film.

- The film was made on a modest budget of $70,000.

- Unlike Romero's other films, this one does not delve into zombie apocalypse or supernatural horror.

- The film is described as a quasi-existentialist counterculture love story.

Reception and Legacy

The Film received mixed reviews upon its release. Some critics appreciated Romero's attempt to explore different genres and tackle social issues, while others felt that the film lacked the impact and originality of his horror works. Despite its mixed reception, "There's Always Vanilla" remains an intriguing entry in Romero's filmography, showcasing his versatility as a filmmaker.

Reflection on "There's Always Vanilla"

In hindsight, "There's Always Vanilla" can be seen as a crucial stepping stone in Romero's career. It allowed him to explore different storytelling techniques and expand his creative boundaries. While the film may not have garnered the same level of acclaim as his horror works, it serves as evidence to Romero's willingness to take risks and challenge himself as a filmmaker.

In the vast realm of George A. Romero's filmography, it's one film often overlooked and yet still manages to captivate a dedicated following. Released between Romero's iconic zombie films, this lesser-known gem holds a distinct allure that continues to resonate with viewers. Despite its initial reception and subsequent obscurity, let us explore the possible reasons why folks still connect with "There's Always Vanilla."

First and foremost, "There's Always Vanilla" showcases Romero's versatility as a filmmaker. Departing from the horror genre he is renowned for, Romero ventured into romantic comedy-drama territory with this film. This unexpected shift attracted a different audience, drawn to the director's exploration of human relationships and societal norms. By delving into the complexities of love, ambition, and the pursuit of happiness, Romero demonstrated his ability to tackle diverse storytelling themes.

Another reason for the enduring appeal of "There's Always Vanilla" is its reflection of the turbulent times in which it was made. Released during the height of the counterculture movement and the Vietnam War, the film captures the zeitgeist of the era. It delves into the generational divide, questioning societal expectations and conventional norms. Through the character of Chris, a disillusioned young man, the film explores the clash between the free-spirited ideals of the 1960s and the harsh realities of the 1970s.

The performances in "There's Always Vanilla" contribute to its lasting impact. Raymond Laine, who portrays Chris, brings a sense of authenticity and relatability to the character. His portrayal of a drifting young man, caught between conforming to societal expectations and pursuing his own dreams, strikes a chord with viewers. Judith Streiner, known for her role in Romero's "Night of the Living Dead," delivers a nuanced performance as Lynn, a woman grappling with her own desires and aspirations.

The film's visual style and cinematography also play a role in its enduring intrigue. Romero's use of natural lighting and handheld camera work lends an intimate and realistic feel to the story. This approach allows the audience to immerse themselves in the characters' lives, heightening the emotional connection and resonance.

Additionally, the music in "There's Always Vanilla" deserves recognition for its contribution to the film's appeal. Composed by Robert Strain, the score complements the narrative, evoking a sense of nostalgia and melancholy. The music helps to enhance the emotional impact of key scenes, allowing viewers to become fully immersed in the characters' experiences.

"There's Always Vanilla" possesses a sense of timelessness that defies its initial reception. Despite being less commercially successful and lesser-known than Romero's other works, the film's exploration of universal themes such as love, identity, and societal pressures gives it a relatability that transcends its era. Its examination of human nature and the pursuit of personal fulfillment continues to resonate with audiences seeking stories that reflect their own struggles and aspirations.

The reasons why folks still connect with "There's Always Vanilla" are multifaceted. The film's departure from Romero's horror roots, its reflection of the social climate of the time, compelling performances, visual style, evocative music, and timeless themes all contribute to its enduring intrigue.

Unveiled to the world in the winter of 1971, "There's Always Vanilla" is a captivating romantic comedy that marked a milestone in the illustrious career of director George A. Romero. This cinematic gem, distributed by the renowned Cambist Films, graced the silver screen in December of that year. While specific box office details remain shrouded in mystery, the film's enduring charm continues to captivate audiences.

The film's journey didn't end with its theatrical run. It found a new home in the realm of home video, released on DVD by Something Weird Video and included in the Anchor Bay Entertainment DVD release of Season of the Witch. The film later made its high-definition debut on Blu-ray on March 13, 2018, further solidifying its place in film history.

While "There's Always Vanilla" is known to exist in a single version, it also goes by another name, "The Affair". This intriguing duality adds another layer to its rich history. The film was also featured in a 6-Disc Limited Edition Blu-ray + DVD set titled "George A. Romero Between Night and Dawn", alongside "Season of The Witch" and "The Crazies".

Chapter 3: Season of the Witch (Hungry Wives)

Romero's Exploration of Feminism and Witchcraft

In 1972, George A. Romero delved into the realm of witchcraft and feminism with his film "Season of the Witch," originally titled "Hungry Wives." Departing from the zombie genre that he had become synonymous with, Romero embraced a new subject matter that allowed him to explore themes of female empowerment, societal expectations, and the supernatural.

The Story Unveiled

"Season of the Witch" follows the journey of Joan Mitchell, a housewife living in suburban Pittsburgh. Dissatisfied with her monotonous life and the societal pressures placed upon her, Joan begins to explore witchcraft as a means of finding liberation and self-expression. As she delves deeper into the occult, Joan becomes increasingly empowered, but also faces the consequences of her actions.

A Feminist Perspective

Romero's decision to center the story around a female protagonist navigating the restrictive gender roles of the early 1970s was a bold move. "Season of the Witch" served as a vehicle for Romero to examine the societal expectations placed upon women and the desire for autonomy and self-discovery. The film presents a critical and feminist perspective on the challenges faced by women in a patriarchal society.

Supernatural Elements and Social Commentary

While "Season of the Witch" incorporates elements of witchcraft and the occult, it also serves as a platform for Romero to comment on various social issues. The film touches upon themes of sexual liberation, marital dissatisfaction, and the conformity that stifles individuality. Through the lens of witchcraft, Romero creates an allegory for the struggles faced by women seeking personal and societal transformation.

The 1972 film "Season of the Witch" features a compelling cast of characters, each bringing their unique talents to the screen.

Jan White, a native of New Castle, Pennsylvania, USA, is a remarkable actress whose performances have left an indelible mark on the film industry. Her most notable performance was in the 1972 film "Season of the Witch," where she played the character of Joan Mitchell. The film traces the journey of Joan, a suburban housewife who seeks solace in witchcraft. White's portrayal of Joan, a woman navigating the complexities of suburban life and the allure of the occult, added a layer of depth and complexity to the film.

White's initial hesitation about the script of "Season of the Witch" due to its nudity showcases her commitment to her craft and personal integrity. However, director George A. Romero's assurance of a stand-in convinced her to take on the role, further highlighting her dedication to the art of storytelling.

Raymond Laine, portraying Gregg, was born on April 9, 1936, in Pittsburgh, Pennsylvania, USA. He was an actor and writer, known for his roles in "Sudden Death" (1995), "There's Always Vanilla" (1971), and "The Devil and Sam Silverstein" (1976). He passed away on November 1, 2000. Beyond the silver screen, Laine's influence permeated the theatrical world. He was a stalwart at Pittsburgh's Playhouse of Point Park College, acting professionally for over two decades. His roles as a director and acting coach at the college allowed him to shape the careers of many aspiring actors.

Ann Muffly, who played the character Shirley, was born on May 23, 1926, in Charleston, West Virginia, USA. She was an actress, known for her roles in "Flashdance" (1983), "Season of the Witch" (1972), and "Knightriders" (1981). She passed away on August 15, 2011.

Bill Thunhurst, who played Jack, was born on December 21, 1920, in the USA. He was an actor, known for his roles in "Season of the Witch" (1972), "The Crazies" (1973), and "Kraft Theatre" (1947). He passed away on January 25, 2011.

Each of these actors brought their unique talents and experiences to their roles, contributing to the overall success and enduring appeal of "Season of the Witch". Their performances continue to captivate audiences, making the film a classic in its genre.

Here is some trivia about the 1972 film "Season of the Witch" by George A. Romero:

- The film was originally released as **Hungry Wives**.

• The film's original title was **Jack's Wife**, which could be seen on VHS copies of the film.

• The film was shot with a small crew in 1972 on 16mm film in the North Hills suburbs and Pittsburgh.

• The film suffered from production problems when the original budget of $250,000 was lowered to $100,000.

• When Joan Mitchell, played by Jan White, said the line "I'm a witch" during filming, the overhead ceiling cracked.

• Romero attributed the ceiling crack to heat from the lights, but some people on set were a little spooked by it.

• When Romero was finished with the final edit, nearly half of the film lay on the cutting room floor.

• The name on the MasterCharge card Joan uses to buy her witchcraft supplies is "George A Romero".

• In the years between his legendary "Night of the Living Dead" and "The Crazies", filmmaker George A. Romero was trying NOT to get pigeonholed as a horror director.

• This film is one of his efforts from that era.

• It's not for hardcore horror fans; other than a few nightmare sequences, it barely flirts with that genre.

• According to director George A. Romero, this is the only one of his films he'd like to remake.

• He cited lack of money as a reason for unhappiness with this production as it turned out.

- According to Jan White, Romero shot 4 hours of footage for the film.

- While shooting a scene, Jan White was getting slapped by actor Bill Thunhurst and a light fell on him during one of the takes.

- Jan White was actually recommended to George A. Romero and Jan was a chosen favorite to play the lead role.

- In 1971, After George A. Romero got married, He made this film.

- The house scene was owned by Mr. and Mrs. Clifford Forrest. Their daughter Christine Forrest even helped with production.

- This film marked Jan White's debut.

Reception and Legacy

Upon its release, "Season of the Witch" received a mixed response from audiences and critics. The film's unconventional narrative and fusion of feminism with supernatural elements challenged traditional genre conventions, which polarized viewers. However, over time, "Season of the Witch" has gained recognition for its unique exploration of feminist themes within the horror genre.

Romero's Continued Exploration of Social Issues

"Season of the Witch" stands as a testament to Romero's commitment to pushing boundaries and using horror as a vehicle for social commentary. While the film may not have achieved the same level of recognition as some of Romero's other works, it remains an important entry in his filmography, showcasing his versatility as a filmmaker and his dedication to exploring diverse themes.

In the realm of cinema, certain films possess a magnetic quality that transcends time, captivating audiences for decades. One such film is the 1972 George Romero masterpiece, "Season of the Witch." Despite the passing years, this cult classic continues to hold a special place in the hearts of cinephiles and horror enthusiasts around the world. The reasons for its enduring appeal are manifold, ranging from its thematic depth to its technical brilliance.

At its core, "Season of the Witch" explores the fragility of the human psyche and the dark forces that dwell within. The film delves into the psychological turmoil of its protagonist, Joan Mitchell, as she grapples with the confines of societal norms and her own internal demons. Romero's masterful storytelling and character development allow viewers to empathize with Joan's journey, questioning their own sanity and the boundaries of their reality. This introspective exploration of the human condition is a timeless theme that resonates with audiences across generations.

Furthermore, "Season of the Witch" boasts a visual aesthetic that remains captivating even by today's standards. Romero's use of stark black and white cinematography creates a haunting atmosphere, amplifying the sense of unease and dread. The deliberate pacing and meticulous attention to detail further enhance the film's ability to immerse viewers in its chilling world. The absence of color not only adds to the film's eerie ambiance, but it also allows the audience to focus on the intricate nuances of the narrative, reinforcing its impact.

The film's enduring popularity can also be attributed to its thematic relevance in the context of its release. In 1972, the world was undergoing significant social and cultural changes, with the feminist movement gaining momentum and challenging traditional gender roles. "Season of the Witch" defied conventions by presenting a complex female protagonist who defies societal expectations, exploring themes of female empowerment and the struggle against patriarchal structures. This progressive portrayal of women in horror cinema was ahead of its time and continues to resonate in an era where gender equality remains a pertinent issue.

Additionally, the film's minimalistic yet haunting score adds another layer of intrigue to its appeal. The atmospheric music, composed by Bruce Roberts, enhances the film's tension and heightens the emotional impact of key scenes. The soundtrack perfectly complements the visuals, creating an immersive experience that lingers in the minds of viewers long after the credits roll.

Lastly, the legacy of "Season of the Witch" is perpetuated by its dedicated fanbase and the influential role it played in shaping the horror genre. The film's impact can be seen in subsequent works, inspiring a new wave of independent horror filmmakers who sought to explore unconventional narratives and push the boundaries of the genre. Its cult status and underground reputation have only grown over time, solidifying its place in the annals of horror cinema.

In conclusion, the reasons why people still connect with the 1972 George Romero film "Season of the Witch" are as diverse as they are compelling. Its exploration of psychological depths, timeless visual aesthetic, thematic relevance, haunting score, and lasting influence on the genre have all contributed to its enduring appeal. As long as there are those who seek to delve into the darkest recesses of the human experience, "Season of the Witch" will continue to captivate and fascinate audiences, remaining a witness to the power of cinema to transcend time.

Valentine's Day in 1973, George A. Romero's film "Season of the Witch" embarked on a journey as twisted and intriguing as its plot. Originally released under the title "Hungry Wives" by Jack H. Harris Enterprises, the film's box office performance remains shrouded in mystery due to the lack of available data.

The film's release history is a labyrinth of edits and re-titles. Initially, "Hungry Wives" ran for a lengthy 130 minutes. However, the film was later trimmed down to 104 minutes for foreign distribution and rebranded as "Jack's Wife". After several years, the film re-emerged under its current title, "Season of the Witch".

The film's journey didn't end there. It found its way into homes with a VHS release in 1998, followed by a DVD release by Anchor Bay in 2005. The DVD version was a partly-restored cut running for 104 minutes. In 2018, the film was introduced to the Blu-Ray format by Arrow Films.

Chapter 7: The Crazies: Paranoia and Government Conspiracy

In this chapter, we turn our attention to another compelling film by George A. Romero, "The Crazies." Released in 1973, "The Crazies" explores the themes of paranoia and government conspiracy in the midst of a deadly outbreak. This chapter will delve into the plot, themes, and character development in "The Crazies," highlighting how Romero skillfully weaves a tale of fear and distrust in the face of a chaotic and uncertain world.

The Premise of "The Crazies"

"The Crazies" takes place in the small town of Evans City, Pennsylvania, where a government experiment involving a biological weapon goes awry. The weapon, codenamed "Trixie," is accidentally released into the town's water supply, leading to a rapidly spreading infection that drives people to madness and violence.

The film focuses on the experiences of a group of survivors as they try to make sense of the chaos around them and navigate the dangerous landscape of a town overrun by infected individuals. As the military intervenes and imposes martial law, the survivors find themselves caught in a web of paranoia and government conspiracy.

Paranoia and Distrust

A central theme in "The Crazies" is the pervasive sense of paranoia and distrust that permeates the story. As the infection spreads and the military takes control, the survivors are faced with the question of whom they can trust. The breakdown of societal order and the threat of infection fuel a growing sense of suspicion among the characters, leading to intense psychological tension.

Romero expertly portrays the psychological toll that paranoia takes on both individuals and communities. The fear of infection and the uncertainty of who might be infected drive the survivors to question each other's motives, blurring the line between friend and foe. This theme of paranoia serves as a reflection of the broader anxieties of the era, echoing the prevailing distrust of government institutions during the Vietnam War era.

Government Conspiracy and Control

"The Crazies" also delves into the theme of government conspiracy and control. As the military intervenes in Evans City, their actions become increasingly oppressive and manipulative. The government's attempts to contain the infection and maintain control over the situation lead to questionable decisions and the loss of innocent lives.

Romero's portrayal of the military as a force of authority gone awry taps into the public's growing skepticism towards government institutions during the 1970s. The film raises important questions about the balance between public safety and individual rights, highlighting the potential dangers of unchecked government power in times of crisis.

Character Study: The Survivors

"The Crazies" presents a diverse cast of characters who must confront their fears and navigate the chaos unfolding around them. From the determined and resourceful nurse Judy to the conflicted and morally ambiguous soldier Clank, each character grapples with their own demons and makes difficult choices in the face of the escalating crisis.

Romero's character development allows audiences to become emotionally invested in the survivors' struggles, providing a human perspective amidst the chaos. Through their experiences, the film explores themes of resilience, sacrifice, and the lengths people will go to protect themselves and their loved ones.

The 1973 film "The Crazies" is a cult classic in the horror genre, and its success can be attributed to the talented cast that brought the story to life.

Born in the heartland of America, Lane Carroll was an actress whose performances resonated deeply with audiences. Her most memorable role was in the 1973 film "The Crazies," where she played Judy, a resident of a small town grappling with the effects of a deadly virus. Her portrayal was so authentic that it left audiences on the edge of their seats.

But Carroll's contributions to the film world extended beyond acting. She was a model, gracing the cover of the first issue of National Lampoon magazine. She also ventured into writing, penning a novel titled "Bespelled" that showcased her creative talent.

Carroll's collaborations with renowned directors like Russ Meyer and George A. Romero further enhanced her acting skills and left a lasting impact on her career. These collaborations were a testament to her talent and versatility.

In essence, Lane Carroll was a multifaceted talent whose contributions to the film world were profound. Her performances, particularly in "The Crazies," were unforgettable. Her work as a model and writer showcased her versatility and commitment to the arts. Even after her passing in 2019, her legacy continues to inspire, reminding us of the power of cinema. Her life and career are a compelling narrative that continues to captivate film enthusiasts around the world.

Will MacMillan, a titan of the film industry, was born in the heartland of Steubenville, Ohio, USA. His journey from a small town to the glitz and glamor of Hollywood is a testament to his talent and determination.

In the haunting 1973 film "The Crazies," MacMillan delivered a performance that still echoes in the corridors of cinematic history. He played David, a firefighter and former Green Beret, who finds himself in a battle for survival in a town overrun by a deadly virus. His portrayal was so raw and authentic that it left audiences on the edge of their seats.

But MacMillan was not just an actor. He was a storyteller, a creator. He wore the hats of a producer and director, showcasing his creative genius beyond acting. His involvement in improvisational theater further underlined his commitment to the craft.

MacMillan's legacy in the film world is not just about his performances or his roles behind the scenes. It's about the lives he touched, the careers he influenced, and the art he created. His story is a riveting saga of talent, creativity, and enduring influence in the world of film. Even after his passing in 2015, his work continues to inspire, reminding us of the power of cinema. His life and career are a compelling narrative that continues to captivate film enthusiasts around the world

Harold Wayne Jones, an actor who etched his name in the annals of film history with his riveting performance in the 1973 film "The Crazies." In a world gone mad with a military biological weapon, Jones's character, Clank, stood as a symbol of hope and resilience. His portrayal was so authentic, so raw, that it left audiences spellbound.

Jones's collaboration with the legendary George A. Romero was a masterstroke, allowing him to work with one of the most influential directors of his time. This experience not only enhanced his acting skills but also added a remarkable chapter to his career.

Jones's legacy in the film world is not just about his performances. It's about the lives he touched, the hearts he moved, and the art he created. His work continues to inspire and captivate, leaving an indelible mark on the film industry. His life and career are a compelling narrative that continues to captivate film enthusiasts around the world. His story is a riveting saga of talent, creativity, and enduring influence in the world of film. His narrative is a compelling tale of dedication, versatility, and creativity in the world of film.

Born in the heart of New York, New York, USA, on April 19, 1935, Lloyd Hollar was an actor whose performances resonated deeply with audiences. His most memorable role was in the 1973 film "The Crazies," where he played Colonel Peckem. The film, directed by the legendary George A. Romero, is a chilling tale of a small Pennsylvania town grappling with the aftermath of a military biological weapon. Amidst this chaos, Hollar's character, Colonel Peckem, emerges as a beacon of hope and resilience.

Hollar's performance was not just compelling but also deeply relatable, resonating with audiences and leaving a lasting impression. His collaboration with Romero, one of the most influential directors of his time, further honed his acting skills and added a remarkable facet to his career.

Born in the heartland of East St. Louis, Illinois, USA, on October 15, 1947, Lynn Lowry is an actress whose performances have left a lasting impression on audiences. Her most memorable role was in the 1973 film "The Crazies," where she played Kathy, a resident of a small town grappling with the effects of a deadly virus. Her portrayal was so authentic that it left audiences spellbound.

Emerging from the vibrant cityscape of New York, Richard Liberty carved a niche for himself in the world of cinema. His portrayal of Artie in the 1973 film "The Crazies" was a masterstroke, painting a vivid picture of a man grappling with the chaos unleashed by a deadly virus. His performance was so raw, so real, that it left audiences riveted.

Each of these actors brought their unique talents to "The Crazies", contributing to the film's status as a cult classic in the horror genre. Their performances continue to be appreciated by audiences today.

Cinematic Techniques and Social Commentary

As with his other films, Romero's use of cinematic techniques in "The Crazies" enhances the storytelling and reinforces the underlying social commentary. The film's gritty visual style and handheld camerawork create a sense of immediacy and chaos, immersing viewers in the disorienting and unpredictable world of the infected.

Romero's exploration of paranoia, government control, and the erosion of trust reflects the broader socio-political climate of the time. "The Crazies" serves as a critique of government overreach and the dangers of unchecked power, inviting audiences to question the motives and actions of those in authority.

Some interesting trivia about the 1973 film "The Crazies"

- The film was shot in Evans City, Pennsylvania.

- Many of the movie's bit players were locals; several of the white-suited soldiers were actually high-school students.

- The burning house at the beginning of the film was a bit of serendipity for the film's crew. The local fire department was burning down an old house to practice putting out the fire, and agreed to let the filmmakers set up and film the event.

- No Hollywood stuntmen were used in The Crazies. Local firemen and licensed fireworks professionals handled all of the action sequences, including the creation and employment of blood squibs.

- The budget for The Crazies was approximately $270,000 and it was Romero's first Union film but he also employed a lot of actors from Pittsburgh and non-professionals from Evans City and Zelienople.

- The basis of the film was a script by Romero's friend and co-worker Paul McCollough entitled 'The Mad People'. McCollough gave the script to Romero with his blessing to re-write it and Romero turned out a revised version of it that was made into 'The Crazies'.

- S. William Hinzman, the film's cinematographer, had a cameo as the local who shoots at the fed's operation station.

● George A. Romero had 2 cameos in the film; the first as a local being herded into the high school and the second as the head of the president of the United States seen on a monitor screen.

"The Crazies" is a thought-provoking and intense film that examines the themes of paranoia and government conspiracy in the face of a deadly outbreak. Romero's masterful storytelling and social commentary make it a standout entry in his filmography, capturing the anxieties and fears of its time. As we delve deeper into Romero's filmography, we will continue to explore the diverse range of themes and stories that he brings to the screen.

Even after all these years, this chilling gem continues to mesmerize audiences, weaving its dark magic and leaving an indelible mark on the souls of those who dare to venture into its harrowing world. Let us delve into the reasons behind its enduring fascination and discover why it continues to hold sway over our collective imagination.

At its core, "The Crazies" peels back the layers of human nature, plunging into the very depths of our psyche. It presents a haunting scenario where a government-created virus ravages a small town, transforming its once-innocent inhabitants into mindless, violent beings. Romero, the maestro of horror, skillfully reflects the fears and anxieties that lurk within us all, inviting us to question our own sanity and contemplate the fragility of our own reality. In this exploration of the human condition, we find a profound connection, as we are forced to confront our deepest fears and ponder our own capacity for madness.

Yet, it is not only Romero's masterful storytelling that captivates us, but also his unyielding depiction of chaos and despair. From the moment the film begins, a sense of claustrophobia envelops us, tightening its grip with each passing frame. The relentless pace and visceral imagery serve as a declaration to Romero's directorial prowess, keeping us on the edge of our seats, our hearts racing, and our senses heightened. The impact of this unrelenting assault on our senses resonates deep within, lingering in our minds long after the credits roll.

Beyond its ability to evoke fear, "The Crazies" strikes a chord by delving into themes of government secrecy and the abuse of power. With its release during a time of social unrest and skepticism towards authority, the film struck a nerve, resonating with an audience hungry for narratives that challenged the actions of those in positions of control. Romero's cautionary tale stands as a stark reminder of the potential consequences of unchecked governmental authority, raising ethical questions that continue to haunt us to this day.

It is the film's raw and gritty depiction of violence that adds another layer to its enduring allure. Romero's use of practical effects and authentic portrayals of bloodshed blur the line between fiction and reality, immersing us in a nightmarish world that feels all too tangible. The visceral authenticity not only intensifies our connection to the story but also compels us to confront our own fears and anxieties, inviting us to question the darkness that resides within our own hearts.

"The Crazies" also owes its timeless appeal to the exceptional performances of its cast. Their portrayal of desperation, fear, and the relentless struggle for survival is nothing short of masterful. Through their gripping performances, we find ourselves emotionally invested in their harrowing journey, forging a profound bond that deepens the impact of the film and leaves an indelible imprint on our souls.

The legacy of "The Crazies" lives on through its enduring influence on the horror genre and its dedicated fanbase. Its gritty aesthetic, thought-provoking social commentary, and unflinching portrayal of violence have inspired a new generation of filmmakers, shaping the landscape of contemporary horror cinema. The film's dark legacy continues to thrive, fueled by the passion and devotion of its ardent followers.

The film stands as a recognition of the power of horror cinema to transcend time and touch the very essence of our being. Through its exploration of human nature, unyielding depiction of chaos, thought-provoking social commentary, raw violence, and lasting influence, it has etched itself into the annals of cinematic history. As long as there are those who seek to be simultaneously terrified and introspective, "The Crazies" will continue to hold sway, reminding us of the fragile nature of our world and the depths of our own humanity.

"The Crazies" opened on March 16, 1973, and was distributed by Cambist Films, the film initially stumbled at the box office, garnering a modest $143,784. Yet, like a phoenix rising from the ashes, it cultivated a dedicated cult following.

The film's journey didn't end there. As the years rolled on, "The Crazies" found new life in various formats. It first graced the VHS format in the late 20th century, courtesy of Anchor Bay. The dawn of the new millennium saw its release on DVD on April 29, 2003, by Blue Underground. Not to be left behind in the high-definition era, the film was introduced to Blu-ray audiences on February 23, 2010. The film's enduring appeal led to a new 4K restoration by Arrow Video, released as part of a box set entitled George A. Romero: Between Night and Dawn, and later as a standalone release on March 13, 2018.

The tale of "The Crazies" is one of reinvention. Despite its initial box office failure, the film's cult status led to a remake in 2010, with Romero himself serving as an executive producer. Thus, the legacy of "The Crazies" lives on, a testament to the enduring appeal of Romero's vision and the power of cinema to captivate audiences across generations and formats.

Chapter 4: The Amusement Park: See you at the park one day!

Romero's Forgotten Gem

"The Amusement Park" is a hidden gem in George A. Romero's filmography. Created in 1973 as a commissioned project for the Lutheran Service Society of Western Pennsylvania, this rarely seen experimental film tackles themes of ageism, societal neglect, and the plight of the elderly in a deeply thought-provoking way.

The Story Unveiled

"The Amusement Park" follows an elderly man as he navigates through a surreal and nightmarish amusement park. Through a series of unsettling encounters and disturbing situations, the film shines a light on the mistreatment and neglect faced by the elderly in society. Romero uses the amusement park setting as a metaphor for the challenges and injustices that older individuals often experience.

The 1975 film "The Amusement Park" is a unique piece of cinema that brought together a diverse group of actors to create a compelling narrative.

Lincoln Maazel, a New York City native born to Russian Jewish parents in 1903, was a multifaceted performer whose influence in the film world is undeniable. His journey into the performing arts began at the tender age of 17 when he was chosen to perform at the Shubert Theater on Broadway, setting the stage for his later work in film.

Despite his early exposure to the performing arts, Maazel didn't venture into acting until he was 56. He graced various theaters with his presence, including the Pittsburgh Playhouse, the Civic Light Opera, and the White Barn Theatre, showcasing his versatility and talent.

Maazel's most notable roles were in George A. Romero's films, particularly "Martin" and "The Amusement Park". In "The Amusement Park", commissioned by the Lutheran Service Society of Western Pennsylvania as an educational film about elder abuse, Maazel played the main character, an elderly man navigating the challenges of aging in America.

His performance, marked by disorientation and isolation amidst chaotic crowds and roller coasters, offered a poignant commentary on society's treatment of the elderly. Beyond his acting roles, Maazel's impact on audiences and the film industry has been profound, contributing to the discourse on societal issues like elder abuse.

In summary, Lincoln Maazel's influence on the film world is significant and enduring. From his early days on Broadway to his impactful roles in film, Maazel's performances continue to resonate with audiences, shedding light on societal issues and enriching the film industry. His legacy is a testament to his talent, versatility, and dedication to his craft.

Each of these actors brought their unique talents to "The Amusement Park", contributing to the film's status as a unique piece in the horror genre. Their performances continue to be appreciated by audiences today.

A Social Commentary

Romero's "The Amusement Park" serves as a powerful social commentary on ageism and the marginalization of the elderly. The film portrays the struggles faced by the protagonist as he is mistreated, ignored, and taken advantage of by those around him. Romero urges viewers to confront the uncomfortable realities of how society often disregards and dismisses the elderly, highlighting the need for compassion and understanding.

Experimental Filmmaking

"The Amusement Park" stands out as an experimental film within Romero's body of work. Departing from his more well-known horror films, Romero takes a creative and unconventional approach in this project. The film features a nonlinear narrative structure, surreal imagery, and a haunting atmosphere that adds to its overall impact. Romero's willingness to experiment with different storytelling techniques showcases his versatility as a filmmaker.

Rediscovery and Recognition

For many years, "The Amusement Park" remained largely unknown, with limited screenings and availability. However, in recent years, the film has gained attention and recognition, leading to its restoration and wider distribution. This newfound appreciation for "The Amusement Park" allows audiences to experience a lesser-known side of Romero's filmmaking and appreciate the depth of his social commentary.

"The Amusement Park" serves as proof to Romero's commitment to using his craft to shed light on societal issues. Even in a commissioned project, Romero managed to infuse his unique perspective and social consciousness. The film stands as a reminder of his dedication to exploring meaningful themes and challenging societal norms through his work.

Trivia about the "The Amusement Park"

- The film was shot in 1973 but went largely unseen for many years.

- It was commissioned by the Lutheran Society, but after seeing Romero's disturbing interpretation of the subject, they were so shocked that they hid the film and it was not shown to anyone.

- A print of the film was rediscovered in 2017 and sent to Romero just three weeks before he passed away.

- The film received a 4K restoration and was acquired by the horror streaming service Shudder in February 2021 for release later that summer.

- Despite representing a person near the end of life in 1973, the main actor didn't pass away until 2009, 36 years later, at the age of 106.

- The film was shot on 16mm film stock at the now-defunct West View Park in West View, Pennsylvania.

- Throughout the movie, there are many scenes where the background music was from Romero's 1978 movie, "Dawn of the Dead".

"The Amusement Park" may not be as widely recognized as some of Romero's other films, but it is a significant addition to his filmography. The film's exploration of ageism and its experimental approach make it a distinctive and thought-provoking piece of cinema. As it continues to gain recognition, "The Amusement Park" reveals another layer of Romero's talent and his ability to create meaningful and impactful stories.

"The Amusement Park" is not just a film; it is an enigma wrapped in celluloid, enticing viewers with its timeless appeal. One of the key factors contributing to its enduring enchantment lies in its ability to transcend the confines of its era. Despite being crafted over four decades ago, the themes explored within the film remain as relevant today as they were then. Romero masterfully delves into profound societal issues, such as ageism, loneliness, and the dehumanization of the elderly. Through the lens of the amusement park, he forces us to confront our own mortality and the fleeting nature of existence. It serves as a stark reminder that life is not always the joyous ride we hope for, despite the allure and excitement that amusement parks promise.

Within the confines of "The Amusement Park," Romero's genius lies in his mastery of visual storytelling. Each frame is meticulously crafted to evoke a sense of unease, a haunting atmosphere that lingers long after the credits roll. The dilapidated amusement park itself becomes a character, a symbol of the decay that accompanies the passage of time. Its cracked paint, broken rides, and faded smiles mirror the fragility and imperfections of our own lives. Romero's ability to invoke fear and discomfort through subtle nuances and surreal visuals is a testament to his unparalleled filmmaking prowess.

"The Amusement Park " has also garnered a devoted cult following, vindication to its enduring allure. Over the years, this passionate community has kept the film alive, organizing screenings, discussions, and even creating their own art inspired by its enigmatic world. The film's cult status adds an element of mystique and intrigue, drawing new audiences who are compelled to experience the magic and unravel its hidden layers. It is an assertion of the power of art to transcend time, connecting individuals across generations who are captivated by its unique blend of horror, social commentary, and thought-provoking storytelling.

Its ability to resonate with audiences decades after its creation is evidence to its profound impact on the human psyche. By exploring universal themes, embracing visual storytelling, and cultivating a devoted cult following, George Romero's masterpiece continues to captivate and bewitch, inviting us to reflect upon the complexities of the human experience. "The Amusement Park" is not merely a film; it is an enduring enchantment, forever etched in the annals of cinematic history, and forever captivating the hearts and minds of those who dare to enter its timeless realm.

Conceived in 1973 and premiered at the American Film Festival in New York in June 1975, the film was originally commissioned by the Lutheran Service Society of Western Pennsylvania as a stark commentary on elder abuse. However, it was shelved shortly after its completion.

For decades, "The Amusement Park" was considered lost to time, its reels gathering dust in some forgotten corner. That is, until 2017, when a 16mm print was unearthed, sparking a resurgence of interest in this once-forgotten gem.

The film was lovingly restored to a 4K version, which had its premiere in Pittsburgh on October 12, 2019. The streaming giant Shudder recognized the film's significance and acquired the distribution rights for North America, the United Kingdom, Ireland, Australia, and New Zealand. On June 8, 2021, the film was made available to a whole new generation of viewers on Shudder.

But the journey of "The Amusement Park" didn't stop there. In a nod to the nostalgia of physical media, the film was released on DVD, Blu-ray, and digital media. Fans eagerly awaited the release of the DVD and Blu-ray versions, which hit the shelves on September 13th, 2022. A limited edition VHS version was also produced, adding to the film's allure.

Today, two versions of "The Amusement Park" exist: the original 1973 version and the 4K restored version. Each version stands as a demonstration to the film's tumultuous history and its enduring appeal.

Chapter 6 - Martin: Exploring the Dark Side of Obsession

"Martin" Released in 1976, "Martin" is a psychological horror film that takes a departure from Romero's more famous zombie films and instead focuses on the internal struggles of its titular character. In this chapter, we will explore the themes, plot, and character development in "Martin," shedding light on how Romero masterfully crafts a haunting tale of obsession and identity.

The Premise of "Martin"

"Martin" centers around the life of Martin Mathias, a young man who believes he is a vampire. However, unlike traditional vampires, Martin lacks supernatural powers and immortality. Instead, he resorts to sedation and razor blades to drink the blood of his victims. The film follows Martin's constant struggle with his identity, his unquenchable desire for blood, and his complex interactions with his dysfunctional family.

Romero's decision to present Martin as a non-traditional vampire sets the stage for a more profound exploration of the human psyche. By stripping away the fantastical elements typically associated with vampires, Romero allows audiences to focus on Martin's internal turmoil and the darker aspects of his obsession.

Exploring the Themes of Isolation and Alienation

A prevalent theme in "Martin" is the overwhelming sense of isolation and alienation experienced by the main character. Martin feels disconnected from the world around him, believing that he is an outsider. This feeling is further amplified by his inability to form meaningful relationships and his internal conflict with his vampiric nature.

Romero skillfully portrays the psychological torment arising from this isolation, forcing viewers to confront their own feelings of loneliness and otherness. Through Martin's experiences, the film explores the universal human desire for connection and the consequences of failing to find it.

The Dichotomy of Reality and Fantasy

Throughout "Martin," Romero blurs the lines between reality and fantasy, leaving audiences questioning the true nature of Martin's vampiric condition. Is Martin truly a vampire, or is he simply a disturbed individual suffering from a delusion? This ambiguity adds to the film's unsettling atmosphere, challenging viewers to question their own perceptions of reality.

Romero's exploration of this dichotomy highlights the thin line between what is real and what is imagined, ultimately leaving audiences in a state of unease. By blurring these boundaries, the film raises thought-provoking questions about the nature of identity and the power of the mind.

Character Study: Martin Mathias

Martin Mathias serves as a complex and enigmatic character, whose struggles form the core of the film. Romero presents Martin as a troubled individual, torn between his insatiable desire for blood and his longing for genuine human connection. As the story unfolds, viewers are given glimpses into Martin's traumatic past, shedding light on the origins of his obsession.

Romero's nuanced portrayal of Martin allows audiences to empathize with his internal conflicts while simultaneously questioning the morality of his actions. Through Martin's character, the film delves into the complexities of the human psyche and the ways in which trauma can shape one's identity.

The Cinematic Style of "Martin"

In "Martin," Romero showcases his prowess as a filmmaker, employing various techniques to create a haunting and atmospheric experience. The use of black and white cinematography adds to the film's bleak and gritty tone, while the realistic settings enhance the overall sense of unease.

Romero also incorporates dream sequences and surreal imagery throughout the film, further blurring the lines between reality and fantasy. These stylistic choices immerse viewers in Martin's disturbed mindset and contribute to the film's overall atmospheric quality.

John Amplas, a name synonymous with the world of film and theater, has left an indelible mark on the industry. Born on June 23, 1949, Amplas first stepped into the limelight with his mesmerizing performance in the cult film "Martin " (1977), directed by George A. Romero. His portrayal of a man convinced of his vampiric nature was so compelling that it led Romero to rewrite the character to suit Amplas's unique acting style.

Amplas's collaboration with Romero didn't end with "Martin". He showcased his versatility in a series of films such as "Dawn of the Dead" (1978), "Knightriders" (1981), "Creepshow" (1982), and "Day of the Dead" (1985). Whether it was playing a Hispanic gang member, a zombie, or a biker, Amplas breathed life into each character, making them memorable.

His performances often tread the delicate balance between the deadly instincts of his characters and the empathy he evokes for them. This is particularly evident in "Martin", where his portrayal of a troubled teenager keeps the audience guessing till the very end.

Beyond the silver screen, Amplas has also made significant contributions to the world of theatre. As a founding member and the Associate Artistic Director of the Pittsburgh Playhouse Repertory Company, he has directed and acted in numerous stage productions. His portrayal of Ricky Roma in David Mamet's "Glengarry Glen Ross" is particularly noteworthy.

Amplas's influence extends to academia as well. As an Associate Professor at Point Park University's Conservatory of Performing Arts, he imparts his wealth of knowledge and experience to the next generation of actors.

Lincoln Maazel, born on February 12, 1903, was an American singer and actor of stage and screen. His journey began at the tender age of 17, performing at the Shubert Theater on Broadway. In "Martin", he played 'Cuda', a character that he infused with depth and intensity.

Christine Forrest, also known as Chris Romero, is a luminary in the film industry. Her journey began on the set of "Season of the Witch", where she met director George A. Romero. This encounter sparked a series of collaborations that would define her career.

In the 1977 film "Martin", Forrest delivered a captivating performance as Christina, a character specifically crafted for her by Romero. Despite being a victim of Martin's vampiric tendencies, Christina's compassion and understanding shine through, offering a safe haven for the troubled protagonist.

Forrest's contributions to the film world extend beyond her acting prowess. She wore multiple hats in "Dawn of the Dead" (1978), showcasing her skills not only as an actress but also as a producer and assistant director. Her versatility and dedication to her craft are evident in her body of work.

From acting to directing and producing, she continues to leave an indelible mark on the industry, creating memorable films that resonate with audiences worldwide. Her enduring collaborations with George A. Romero has resulted in a legacy that continues to inspire future generations of filmmakers.

Tom Savini, a name that resonates in the realm of film, is renowned for his multifaceted contributions to the industry. However, his acting prowess, particularly in the 1977 film "Martin", truly stands out.

In "Martin", Savini took on the role of Arthur, a supporting character. This marked his first collaboration with director George A. Romero, setting the stage for a series of successful partnerships. Savini's portrayal of Arthur was compelling, adding depth to the narrative and enhancing the overall cinematic experience.

While Savini is celebrated for his groundbreaking work in prosthetic makeup and special effects, his performance in "Martin" showcased his versatility. His ability to breathe life into his character contributed significantly to the film's success and left a lasting impression on audiences.

In essence, Tom Savini's performance in "Martin" is a testament to his acting talent. His portrayal of Arthur not only enriched the film but also highlighted his versatility as an artist. His work continues to inspire, leaving an indelible mark on the film industry. We will discuss Tom much much more in this book.

Critical Reception and Legacy

Upon its release, "Martin" received mixed reviews from critics, with some praising its psychological depth and others finding it too disturbing. However, over the years, the film has gained a cult following and is now recognized as one of Romero's most thought-provoking works.

Trivia about the 1977 film "Martin"

- The original cut of the film ran nearly 2 hours 45 minutes. As of 2021, this version has never been screened publicly and was considered lost until it was rediscovered through the efforts of Romero scholar Kevin Kriess and The Living Dead Museum.

• Often said to be George A. Romero's personal favorite of his films.

• Romero's original script for the film had the character of Martin as an older person who was actually established as a vampire struggling to live in a modern world. However, when Romero saw John Amplas' performance on stage he re-wrote the character with Amplas in mind, making Martin a younger and more innocent character.

• According to producer Richard P. Rubinstein on the Dawn of the Dead (1978) commentary track (Ultimate Edition DVD), by the time both he and George A. Romero got together to make this film, Romero was under a serious debt (almost a million dollars) after the back to back failures of the films he'd done after Night of The Living Dead (1968). Rubinstein told Romero it was alright to declare bankruptcy and start over again. However Romero refused because he felt it was inappropriate to back out on the people who had helped invest in Romero's films. Rubinstein, having a lot of respect for Romero for not walking out on those people, partnered up with him so he could help him get out of his debt. This was their first film together but it wasn't until they made Dawn of the Dead, which became a financial success, that they were able to pay back Romero's debts.

• Director George A. Romero originally wanted the entire film to be in black and white, but the producers didn't want to risk this experiment and insisted that the majority of the film be in color.

"Martin" continues to captivate audiences to this day for several compelling reasons. Despite being over four decades old, the movie's themes, characters, and unique approach to storytelling remain relevant and thought-provoking. "Martin" matters because it delves deep into the complexities of human nature, exploring the blurred lines between reality and fantasy, as well as the innate desire for connection and understanding.

At its core, "Martin" presents a profoundly ambiguous protagonist who struggles with his identity and purpose. The titular character, Martin, believes he is a vampire, but the film challenges the audience to question the authenticity of his claim. This ambiguity raises intriguing questions about the nature of truth and perception. Is Martin truly a vampire, or is he merely a troubled individual seeking an escape from his mundane existence? The film invites viewers to contemplate the thin line between delusion and reality, leaving room for personal interpretation and introspection.

Moreover, "Martin" skillfully explores the human longing for connection. Martin, despite his questionable nature, is a lonely and isolated character. He yearns for companionship and human connection, which resonates with audiences who have experienced similar feelings of alienation. Romero portrays Martin as a sympathetic figure, highlighting the universal human need for understanding and acceptance. By doing so, the film challenges societal norms and prejudices, reminding us that compassion and empathy should not be reserved only for those who fit societal expectations.

Another reason why "Martin" continues to captivate viewers is its unconventional approach to the vampire genre. Unlike traditional vampire films, Romero eschews supernatural elements and instead focuses on the psychological and emotional aspects of vampirism. By stripping away the mythical tropes, Romero portrays vampirism as a metaphor for addiction or mental illness. This unique perspective adds depth to the story, prompting discussions about the nature of addiction, the struggles of mental health, and the societal stigmas surrounding these issues.

Furthermore, "Martin" stands out for its gritty and realistic portrayal of urban decay. Set in a declining Pittsburgh neighborhood, the film serves as a social commentary on the deteriorating urban landscape and the accompanying sense of hopelessness. Romero's use of stark visuals and atmospheric cinematography effectively captures the bleakness and desolation of the setting, reflecting the marginalized lives of the characters. This raw depiction of society's underbelly resonates with audiences, sparking conversations about poverty, inequality, and the effects of urban decay on individuals and communities.

The film's ambiguity, relatable characters, and thought-provoking themes continue to captivate audiences, prompting them to reflect on their own lives and the world around them. "Martin" serves as a reminder that great storytelling transcends time, and its impact will continue to be felt for generations to come.

"Martin" is a masterpiece that still matters because it makes us question our own reality. The film challenges the norm and offers a fresh perspective on the vampire genre. Martin's ambiguous character forces us to ponder the frailty of our own beliefs and question the boundaries of our existence. Is he truly a vampire, or is he a victim of his own delusions? The film leaves us with no easy answers, forcing us to confront the complexities of human nature and the blurred lines between fantasy and reality.

Beyond its profound exploration of identity, "Martin" also delves into the universal human desire for connection. Martin's loneliness and yearning for companionship resonate deeply with audiences. Romero presents him as a sympathetic figure, highlighting the importance of empathy and understanding for those who are marginalized or different. By doing so, the film challenges societal norms and prejudices, urging us to embrace compassion and reject judgment.

What sets "Martin" apart from other vampire films is its gritty and realistic portrayal of urban decay. Romero's decision to set the film in a declining Pittsburgh neighborhood adds a layer of social commentary. The bleak visuals and atmospheric cinematography capture the despair and desolation of the setting, reflecting the struggles faced by the characters. This raw depiction of society's underbelly forces us to confront issues of poverty, inequality, and the effects of urban decay on individuals and communities.

In essence, "Martin" remains relevant because it defies conventions and challenges our perceptions. It encourages us to question the nature of truth, the importance of connection, and the impact of societal decay. The film's ambiguity and thought-provoking themes make it a timeless masterpiece that continues to resonate with audiences across generations. "Martin" is a manifestation using the power of cinema to evoke introspection and spark conversations about the human condition.

Opening to audiences in September 1977, this film was brought to life by the distribution efforts of Libra Films. "Martin" was initially captured on 16mm in the Super 16 format, a testament to the film-making techniques of the era. It was later introduced to a new generation of horror enthusiasts when Lionsgate released it on DVD on November 9, 2004. The film continued to reach a wider audience when it was released in a two-disc DVD set by Arrow Video in the United Kingdom on June 28, 2010. The anticipation is building as fans eagerly await the film's Blu-Ray release scheduled for March 27, 2023.

The intrigue of "Martin" is further deepened by the existence of two distinct versions. The original theatrical release, running for 95 minutes, is well-known among fans. However, a recently discovered director's cut, a black and white version that spans an epic three and a half hours, has sparked renewed interest.

Chapter 7: Dawn of the Dead: Consumerism and Social Commentary

In this chapter, we will delve into George A. Romero's iconic film, "Dawn of the Dead." Released in 1978, "Dawn of the Dead" further explored the themes of societal decay and social commentary that Romero introduced in "Night of the Living Dead." This film not only continued the legacy of the zombie genre but also offered a biting critique of consumerism and the modern world.

The Plot and Setting

"Dawn of the Dead" takes place in a world overrun by zombies, just like its predecessor. The story follows a group of survivors who seek refuge in a shopping mall, barricading themselves from the outside world and the relentless hordes of the undead. As they navigate through the challenges of survival, the film explores themes of consumerism, isolation, and the erosion of humanity in the face of a zombie apocalypse.

The setting of the shopping mall is symbolic and serves as a backdrop for Romero's critique of consumer culture. The survivors find temporary comfort and security within the mall's confines, but it also becomes a reflection of their own desires and materialistic tendencies. The film cleverly juxtaposes the mindless consumerism of the zombies with the human characters' own struggle to resist the allure of material possessions.

Consumerism and Social Commentary

"Dawn of the Dead" is a scathing critique of consumerism and the excesses of modern society. Romero uses the zombie apocalypse as a metaphor to explore how consumer culture has turned people into mindless zombies, driven by their insatiable desire for material possessions. The zombies in the film are drawn to the mall, instinctively seeking the familiar comfort of their former lives as consumers.

Romero's portrayal of the survivors' interactions with the mall's various stores and merchandise highlights the emptiness and futility of consumerism. Despite being surrounded by material wealth, the characters struggle to find meaning and fulfillment in their lives. The film suggests that consumerism has eroded their humanity, leaving them hollow and disconnected from each other.

Gore and Satire

"Dawn of the Dead" is also notable for its explicit and graphic depiction of violence and gore. Romero's use of practical effects and gruesome makeup created a visceral and shocking experience for audiences. However, the violence in the film serves a purpose beyond mere shock value.

Romero employs gore and violence as a satirical tool, highlighting the absurdity and brutality of the world he has created. By exaggerating the violence, he forces the audience to confront the ugliness of humanity and the consequences of unchecked consumerism. The film's blend of horror and satire makes it a unique and unforgettable entry in the zombie genre.

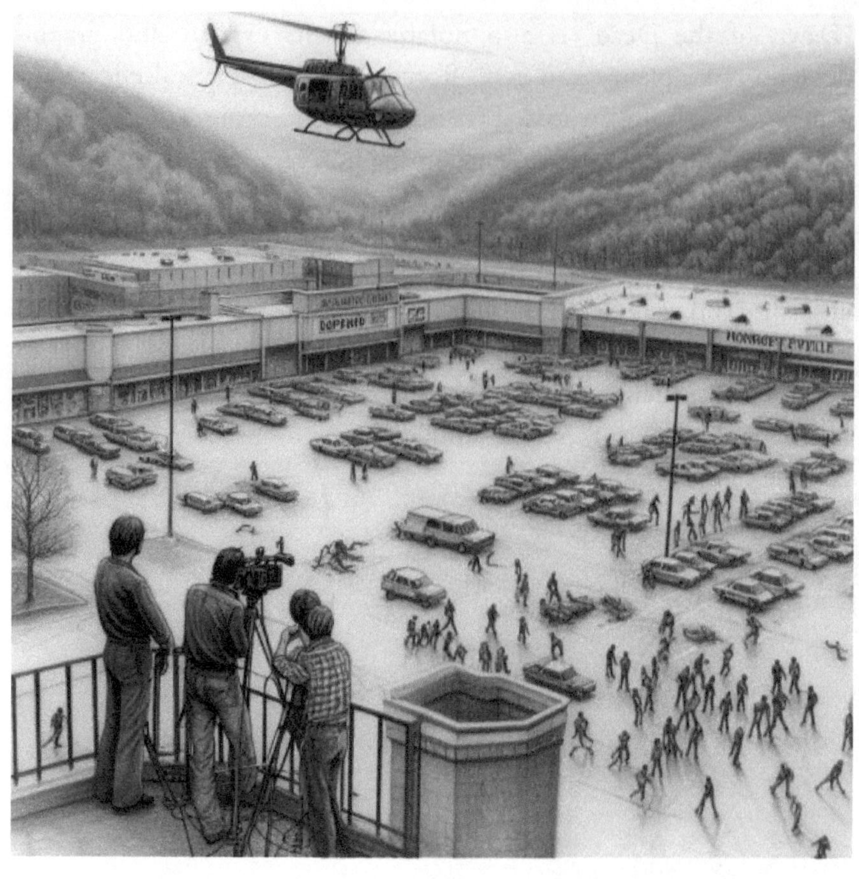

"Dawn of the Dead" (1978) is a classic horror film that brought together a talented cast of actors who brought life into their characters, making the film a memorable piece of cinema.

David Emge, an American actor born on September 9, 1946, in Evansville, Indiana, is best known for his role as Stephen in the 1978 horror film "Dawn of the Dead". Emge's journey from a chef in a New York City restaurant to an actor is a testament to his passion for the arts. His performance in "Dawn of the Dead" is considered one of the best portrayals of a zombie ever seen on screen.

Despite having a limited filmography, Emge's impact on the horror genre is significant. His roles in films like "Basket Case 2" and "Hellmaster" further showcase his acting prowess. Apart from his film roles, Emge has also made significant contributions to live theater.

Emge may not have an extensive list of film credits, but his influence on the film industry, particularly the horror genre, is undeniable. His memorable performance in "Dawn of the Dead" continues to be a benchmark in horror cinema, making him a notable figure in film history.

Kentotis Alvin Foree, known as Ken Foree, is an American actor who has made significant contributions to the film world. Born on February 29, 1948, in Indianapolis, Indiana, Foree is best recognized for his role as Peter in the 1978 horror film "Dawn of the Dead". His performance in this film was not only impressive but also contributed to the film's success and its status as a classic in the horror genre.

Foree's acting career, which began in the 1970s, is marked by a variety of roles in different genres. He has demonstrated his versatility in films like "Knightriders" (1981), "From Beyond" (1986), and "Leatherface: Texas Chainsaw Massacre III" (1990). His contributions also extend to television, where he played Roger Rockmore on the Nickelodeon sitcom "Kenan & Kel" and made guest appearances on a range of TV shows.

In addition to his acting roles, Foree has also made significant contributions as a producer and writer. His influence is evident in the next generation of filmmakers, with references to him in films like the horror-comedy "Shaun of the Dead".

In summary, Ken Foree's contributions to the film world are both significant and varied. His performances have not only entertained audiences but also inspired other actors and filmmakers. His legacy continues to influence the film world, making him a notable figure in film history.

Scott Hale Reiniger, an American actor born on September 5, 1948, is best known for his role as Roger in the horror film "Dawn of the Dead". His performance in this film has left a lasting impact on the horror genre. Reiniger's acting career, which began after graduating from Rollins College in Theater Arts, is marked by a variety of roles in different genres.

In addition to his acting roles, Reiniger has made significant contributions to theater and film production. He has worked extensively with playwrights and has studied Film and Television Production and Cinematography at various institutions. Currently, he heads the Camera Department at The American Academy of Dramatic Arts in Los Angeles.

Reiniger's contributions to the film world are both significant and varied. His memorable performance in "Dawn of the Dead" and his work in theater and film production have left a lasting impact on the industry.

Gaylen Ross, an American actress born on August 15, 1950, is best known for her role as Francine Parker in the 1978 horror film "Dawn of the Dead". After her acting career, Ross transitioned into directing and producing, making significant contributions to the film world.

Ross studied at Monterey Peninsula College and The New School for Social Research, and was the managing editor of the literary journal Antaeus and Ecco Press. Her documentary films, including "Killing

Kasztner" and "Dealers Among Dealers", have been well-received. Ross' company, GR Films, has produced several documentaries that have left a lasting impact on the industry.

In addition to her work in film and television, Ross co-authored "Married To A Stranger", a book about the Russian mail order bride business. Her unique lineage and diverse contributions to the film industry make her a notable figure in film history.

Each of these actors brought their unique talents to the film, contributing to its status as a classic in the horror genre. Their performances remain etched in the minds of viewers, making "Dawn of the Dead" a film that continues to be celebrated decades after its release.

"Dawn of the Dead" solidified George A. Romero's status as a master of horror and further cemented the popularity of the zombie genre. The film's social commentary and critique of consumerism continue to resonate with audiences, even decades after its release.

● Filming Locations: The movie was primarily filmed in the Monroeville Mall located in Monroeville, Pennsylvania.

● Budget Constraints: Real pig intestines were used for the gore scenes.

● Political Commentary: The film critiques consumerism and the mindless pursuit of material possessions.

● Zombie Extras: Local residents were cast as extras to portray the zombies.

- Multiple Versions: Different versions of the film have been released, including the theatrical cut, extended cut, and director's cut.

- Critical Reception: Initially received mixed reviews but has since gained cult status within the zombie genre.

- Box Office Success: Grossed over $55 million worldwide, becoming one of the highest-grossing independent films of its time.

- Talking Zombies: George A. Romero initially envisioned zombies being able to talk in the film.

- Functional Stores: Some stores in the Monroeville Mall were open for business during filming, such as restaurants that closed much later at night.

- Real Bikers: The bikers in the film were actual members of a local motorcycle gang.

Romero's exploration of societal decay and his use of zombies as a metaphor for cultural issues have inspired countless filmmakers and storytellers. "Dawn of the Dead" remains a powerful and influential film that serves as a reminder of the dangers of unchecked consumerism and the fragility of human civilization.

Dawn of the Dead continues to captivate audiences even after several decades since its release. This cult classic has stood the test of time and remains relevant for a myriad of reasons. One of the primary factors contributing to its enduring popularity is its exploration of timeless themes that resonate with viewers. The movie delves into the human condition, the fear of the unknown, and the fragility of society, all of which continue to be relevant in our modern world. Additionally, the film's innovative use of cinematic techniques and its impact on the horror genre have solidified its place in cinematic history.

Set in a post-apocalyptic world overrun by zombies, Dawn of the Dead presents a grim portrayal of society on the brink of collapse. As the survivors take refuge in a shopping mall, the film offers a scathing critique of consumerism and the superficiality of modern life. This commentary on society's obsession with material possessions remains pertinent today, reminding us of the emptiness that can come with excessive consumerism.

Moreover, the film's portrayal of the human condition and the complex dynamics between its characters strikes a chord with audiences. The survivors represent a microcosm of society, each grappling with their own fears, desires, and flaws. This exploration of human nature and the moral dilemmas faced in extreme circumstances provokes contemplation on our own values and actions. Dawn of the Dead forces us to question how we would respond in a similar situation, challenging our notions of morality and empathy.

The movie's ability to evoke fear and suspense is another reason for its enduring appeal. Romero's masterful direction and the practical effects used to create the zombies contribute to the film's visceral impact. The tension builds as the survivors navigate the dangers surrounding them, constantly reminding us of the fragile balance between life and death. The film's iconic scenes, such as the opening sequence in the television studio and the relentless onslaught of the undead, continue to leave audiences on the edge of their seats.

Dawn of the Dead's influence on the horror genre cannot be overstated. The film introduced groundbreaking elements that have become staples of the genre. Romero's use of social commentary within a horror framework inspired countless filmmakers to explore deeper themes in their work. The film's success paved the way for the modern zombie subgenre, with its impact evident in popular television shows like The Walking Dead.

In addition to its thematic depth and cinematic achievements, Dawn of the Dead benefits from a dedicated fanbase that has kept its legacy alive. The film's release coincided with the rise of horror fandom and the emergence of conventions and fan communities. These fans have celebrated and analyzed every aspect of the film, contributing to its enduring popularity through discussions, merchandise, and fan-made content. The movie's cult status has transcended generations, with younger audiences discovering and appreciating its significance.

The reasons for the continued connection with the 1978 George Romero film Dawn of the Dead are abundant. Its exploration of timeless themes, such as the human condition and the fragility of society, its scathing critique of consumerism, and its ability to evoke fear and suspense, have ensured its relevance even after several decades. Furthermore, the film's impact on the horror genre and its dedicated fanbase have solidified its place in cinematic history. Dawn of the Dead continues to matter because it challenges us to confront our own fears, question societal norms, and reflect on the human experience in a way that few films can achieve.

Dawn of the Dead has become a cult favorite for numerous reasons. Firstly, it taps into our fascination with the apocalyptic and the undead. The film presents a scenario in which the world has descended into chaos, and the dead rise to feast on the living. This concept of a post-apocalyptic world, filled with terrifying zombies, resonates with our primal fears and curiosity about the unknown.

Additionally, the film's gritty and realistic portrayal of the zombie outbreak makes it feel plausible, adding to its allure. The special effects, although primitive by today's standards, still hold up and create a sense of dread and tension. The grotesque makeup and practical effects used to bring the zombies to life contribute to the film's visceral impact and make it a visual feast for horror enthusiasts.

Dawn of the Dead offers a unique blend of horror and social commentary. By setting the film primarily in a shopping mall, Romero cleverly critiques consumerism and the mindless pursuit of material possessions. The survivors' desperate attempts to find safety and comfort within a place of consumer excess serve as a metaphor for society's obsession with consumer culture. This underlying social commentary adds depth to the film and elevates it beyond a mere horror flick.

The characters in Dawn of the Dead are relatable and well-developed, which further enhances the film's appeal. From the tough and resourceful Fran to the conflicted and morally ambiguous Roger, each character brings a different perspective to the narrative. Audiences become emotionally invested in their survival, rooting for their resilience in the face of overwhelming odds.

Another reason for the film's enduring popularity is its influence on the horror genre. Dawn of the Dead revolutionized the zombie subgenre, introducing the concept of slow-moving, flesh-eating zombies that has become a staple in popular culture. Countless films, television shows, and video games have since followed in its footsteps, paying homage to Romero's groundbreaking work.

The fan community surrounding Dawn of the Dead has played a significant role in keeping the film's legacy alive. Fans have passionately embraced the film, organizing conventions, creating fan art, and engaging in lively discussions about its themes and symbolism. The film's enduring popularity can be attributed, in part, to the dedication and enthusiasm of its fanbase.

The reasons why folks still connect with the 1978 George Romero film Dawn of the Dead are diverse and multi-faceted. Its exploration of the apocalyptic, the blend of horror and social commentary, the relatable characters, its influence on the genre, and the passionate fan community all contribute to its continued relevance. Dawn of the Dead has secured its place as a classic in the horror genre, captivating audiences with its terrifying zombies, thought-provoking themes, and enduring impact.

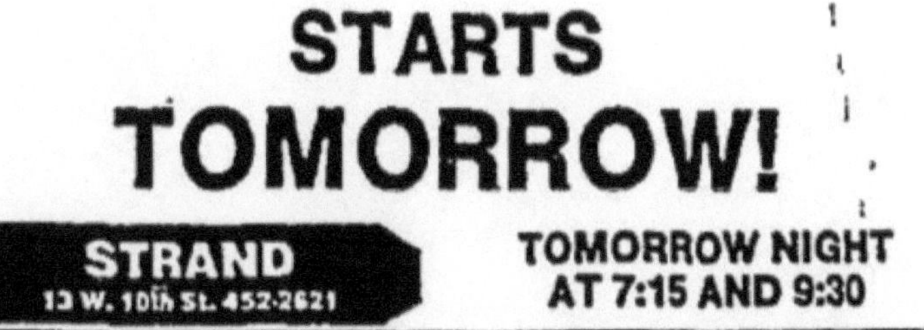

This iconic film first terrified audiences in Italy on September 1, 1978, before making its way across the globe. The film was distributed by the United Film Distribution Company in the US and Titanus in Italy, and it quickly became a sensation, sending chills down the spines of viewers worldwide.

Despite its modest budget of $640,000, "Dawn of the Dead" proved to be a box office juggernaut, grossing a staggering $66 million worldwide. This success underscored the film's enduring appeal and the universal allure of its chilling narrative.

Chapter 8: Knightriders: Fighting the Dragon

Romero's Unique Departure into Medieval Fantasy

In 1981, George A. Romero took a departure from the horror genre and ventured into the world of medieval fantasy with his film "Knightriders." This unconventional and often overlooked film showcases Romero's versatility as a filmmaker, as he crafts a tale of chivalry, honor, and the struggle to maintain integrity in a changing world.

The Modern-Day Knights

"Knightriders" introduces us to a modern-day traveling troupe of motorcycle-riding performers who have adopted the code of knights from the medieval era. Led by the charismatic and determined King Billy, played by Ed Harris in one of his early leading roles, the group reenacts jousting tournaments and other medieval traditions while living a nomadic lifestyle.

Themes of Identity and Integrity

At its core, "Knightriders" is a film about individuality, the pursuit of personal ideals, and the challenges of remaining true to oneself in the face of societal pressures. The characters in the film grapple with their own identities and struggle to balance their commitment to the code of the knights with the realities of the modern world.

A Unique Blend of Genres

"Knightriders" stands out for its fusion of medieval fantasy elements with the contemporary setting of a traveling carnival. Romero seamlessly combines the two worlds, creating a thought-provoking narrative that explores themes of tradition, rebellion, and the clash between the old and the new. The film's blend of genres adds depth and complexity to the story, showcasing Romero's ability to break away from traditional storytelling conventions.

In the realm of cinematic history, the 1981 film "Knightriders" holds a unique place, largely due to its eclectic and talented cast.

Ed Harris, an American actor renowned for his intense performances, was born on November 28, 1950, in Tenafly, New Jersey. His acting journey began at Columbia University and later at the University of

Oklahoma, where he developed a passion for the craft. He then moved to California and graduated from the California Institute of the Arts in 1975.

His breakthrough came in 1981 with George A. Romero's "Knightriders", where he played Billy, the leader of a troupe of bikers who joust at medieval fairs. This role showcased his ability to portray complex characters and set the stage for his future success.

Harris's career is marked by a diverse range of roles that have earned him critical acclaim and numerous award nominations. His performances in films like "The Right Stuff", "The Abyss", "State of Grace", "Glengarry Glen Ross", "The Firm", "Needful Things", "Nixon", "The Rock", "Stepmom", "A Beautiful Mind", "Enemy at the Gates", "A History of Violence", "Gone Baby Gone", "National Treasure: Book of Secrets", "Snowpiercer", "Mother!", "The Lost Daughter", and "Top Gun: Maverick" demonstrate his remarkable range.

His portrayal of American painter Jackson Pollock in "Pollock", a film he also directed, was highly acclaimed. His performances in "Apollo 13", "The Truman Show", "Pollock", and "The Hours" earned him Academy Award nominations.

Ed Harris's contributions to the film world are significant. His role in "Knightriders" was a stepping stone in his illustrious career, and his work continues to inspire and captivate audiences worldwide. His intense performances, diverse roles, and directorial ventures have left an indelible mark on the industry.

Gary Lahti, an actor born on June 22, 1952, in Albany, New York, is known for his roles in films such as "Knightriders", "A Modern Affair", and "The Runestone". His acting journey began with a Master of Fine Arts from the University of Minnesota.

His breakthrough came in 1981 with George A. Romero's "Knightriders", where he played Alan, a loyal supporter of the troupe's leader, Billy. This role showcased his ability to portray complex characters and set the stage for his future success.

Lahti's career is marked by a diverse range of roles that have earned him critical acclaim. His performances in films like "A Modern Affair" and "The Runestone" demonstrate his remarkable range.

Tom Savini, an acclaimed actor and special effects artist, delivered a memorable performance in George A. Romero's 1981 film "Knightriders". In the film, Savini played Morgan, a member of a traveling renaissance fair troupe. His portrayal of Morgan, a character who becomes discontent with the leadership and covets the crown, added depth to the film's exploration of the tension between idealism and reality. This role showcased Savini's ability to bring complex characters to life, contributing to the film's unique blend of action and drama. His performance as Morgan in "Knightriders" is a testament to his talent and commitment to his craft, leaving a lasting impression on audiences worldwide.

Amy Ingersoll, an actress born in New York City, delivered a memorable performance in George A. Romero's 1981 film "Knightriders". In the film, Ingersoll played Linet, the queen of a traveling renaissance fair troupe. Her portrayal of Linet, a complex character, added depth to the film's exploration of the tension between idealism and reality. This role showcased Ingersoll's ability to bring complex characters to life, contributing to the film's unique blend of action and drama. Her performance as Linet in "Knightriders" is a testament to her talent and commitment to her craft, leaving a lasting impression on audiences worldwide.

Patricia Tallman, an accomplished actress, stunt performer, and studio executive, has made significant contributions to the film world. Born on September 4, 1957, in Pontiac, Illinois, USA, Tallman's career spans several decades, with notable roles in films and television series that have left an indelible mark on the industry.

Tallman's journey into acting began at a young age, and her passion for the craft led her to pursue a career in the film industry. Over the years, she has demonstrated her versatility as an actress, taking on a variety of roles that showcase her range and talent.

One of Tallman's most memorable roles was in George A. Romero's 1981 film "Knightriders", where she played the character of Julie Dean. The film, which centers around a traveling renaissance fair troupe, allowed Tallman to showcase her ability to portray complex characters. Her character, Julie Dean, is a member of the troupe, and her performance added depth to the film's exploration of the tension between idealism and reality.

Tallman's performance in "Knightriders" was not only delightful but also significant. It contributed to the film's unique blend of action and drama and showcased her ability to bring complex characters to life. Her portrayal of Julie Dean was a significant contribution to the film and demonstrated her talent and commitment to her craft.

Beyond "Knightriders", Tallman has demonstrated her acting skills in other films and television series. She is best known for her roles in "Night of the Living Dead", "Star Trek", and "Babylon 5". Each of these roles has allowed her to showcase her range as an actress and contribute to the richness and diversity of the film and television industry.

Each of these actors brought their unique talents and experiences to their roles in "Knightriders", contributing to the film's enduring appeal. Their diverse backgrounds and careers in the film industry have left a lasting impact on cinema.

The Performances and Legacy

The performances in "Knightriders" are a highlight, with Ed Harris delivering a commanding portrayal of the conflicted King Billy. The ensemble cast, including Tom Savini and Patricia Tallman, also shines, bringing depth and authenticity to their respective roles. While the film did not receive significant commercial success upon its release, it has since gained a cult following and is regarded as a unique entry in Romero's filmography.

Here are some interesting trivia about the 1981 film "Knightriders" by George A. Romero:

- First Cut Duration: The first cut of the movie ran for around a staggering seventeen hours.

- Stephen King's Cameo: Stephen King and his wife Tabitha King played a spectator with a loud mouth opinion and his wife in the first scene at the fair.

- Ed Harris's Role: This film marked the first top-billed lead starring role in a cinema movie of actor Ed Harris.

- Influence and Inspiration: The medieval pre-17th-century Europe tribute organization, the Society for Creative Anachronism, was an influence and inspiration for the movie.

- Title Controversy: The picture debuted in the year preceding the similarly-titled, popular, yet unrelated television series Knight Rider (1982).

- Filming Location: It was filmed entirely on location in the Pittsburgh metro area, including Fawn Township and Natrona during the summer of 1980.

- Genre: The film represents a change of pace for Romero, known primarily for his horror films; it is a personal drama about a traveling renaissance fair troupe.

Romero's Exploration of Personal Ideals

"Knightriders" is a validation to Romero's willingness to explore unconventional narratives and challenge genre expectations. The film reflects his own personal ideals and the constant struggle to maintain integrity in an ever-changing world. While it may not be as well-known as his zombie films, "Knightriders" is a confirmation to Romero's versatility and his ability to tackle diverse subjects with depth and sincerity.

The 1981 George Romero film, "Knightriders," continues to captivate audiences even after four decades since its release. This cult classic holds a special place in the hearts of many, and its enduring appeal can be attributed to several factors.

First and foremost, the movie still matters because of its unique and unconventional premise. "Knightriders" tells the story of a traveling Renaissance fair troupe that reimagines the Arthurian legend with a modern twist. Led by a charismatic and enigmatic figure named King Billy, played by Ed Harris in one of his early breakthrough roles, the troupe portrays knights who joust on motorcycles instead of horses. This innovative concept blends elements of medieval chivalry with the rebellious spirit of the 1980s, creating a fascinating and unexpected narrative.

Furthermore, "Knightriders" resonates with audiences due to its exploration of personal identity and the struggle between conformity and individuality. The characters in the film grapple with the pressures of society and the desire to remain true to themselves. King Billy, in particular, becomes a symbol of defiance, as he refuses to conform to the expectations imposed upon him. This theme of self-discovery and the pursuit of authenticity strikes a chord with viewers, as it reminds them of the ongoing battle to stay true to one's beliefs in a world that often demands conformity.

The film's enduring relevance can also be attributed to its underlying commentary on the clash between commercialization and artistic integrity. "Knightriders" showcases the tension between the noble ideals of the Renaissance fair and the encroaching influence of corporate interests. As the troupe gains popularity and financial success, they face the temptation of selling out their unique vision for the sake of commercial gain. This struggle for artistic integrity is a theme that still resonates strongly today, as many creative individuals find themselves torn between staying true to their artistic vision or compromising for financial stability.

Additionally, the film's timeless appeal lies in its portrayal of friendship, camaraderie, and the power of community. The close-knit group of characters in "Knightriders" forms a surrogate family, bound together by their shared passion and unconventional way of life. Their unwavering support for one another in the face of adversity creates a sense of warmth and belonging that resonates with audiences. In a world where genuine connections are often elusive, the film's depiction of deep friendships and the strength of community strikes a chord and reminds viewers of the importance of human connection.

From its unconventional premise and exploration of personal identity to its commentary on artistic integrity and the power of community, the film resonates with viewers on multiple levels. Moreover, the film's hidden messages hint at a deeper reality that lies beyond the screen. "Knightriders" continues to matter today.

On April 10, 1981, "Knightriders" emerged from the creative genius of George A. Romero. This cinematic gem was brought to audiences across the United States by the United Film Distribution Company and reached international shores through United Artists.

Despite its intriguing premise, "Knightriders" faced a tough battle at the box office. The journey of "Knightriders" didn't end at the theaters. It found a new lease of life in the realm of home media. Although the exact date of its VHS release remains unknown, the film made its DVD debut on July 11, 2000. Later, it was introduced to the Blu-Ray format on November 26, 2013.

Interestingly, "Knightriders" exists in two distinct versions. The original cut, Romero's preferred version, had a runtime of 2 hours and 45 minutes. However, the theatrical release was trimmed down to 145 minutes. This decision was likely driven by the desire to make the film more commercially appealing and accessible to a broader audience. The longer version, often referred to as the "director's cut", offers a deeper dive into Romero's vision.

Chapter 9: Creepshow: A Love Letter to Horror Anthologies

In this chapter, we explore George A. Romero's film "Creepshow," released in 1982. Unlike Romero's previous zombie-themed films, "Creepshow" is an anthology horror film that pays homage to the classic horror comics of the 1950s. With its unique blend of horror, humor, and comic book-style storytelling, "Creepshow" stands as a love letter to the horror anthology genre.

"Creepshow" is composed of five separate stories, each inspired by different horror comic book tales. The film follows a framing narrative featuring a young boy named Billy, who is punished by his strict father for reading horror comics. As Billy seeks revenge, the stories unfold, each with its own distinct tone and style.

The anthology format allows "Creepshow" to explore a variety of horror subgenres, including supernatural revenge, creature features, and dark humor. Each story is presented as a standalone segment, providing a diverse and entertaining viewing experience.

Romero and writer Stephen King drew inspiration from the horror comics of the 1950s, such as "Tales from the Crypt" and "The Vault of Horror." These comics often featured macabre and morality-based stories with twist endings. "Creepshow" captures the spirit of these comics, delivering a nostalgic and visually striking tribute to the genre.

The film replicates the visual style of comic book panels through its use of vibrant colors, bold typography, and exaggerated camera angles. Each segment is introduced with a comic book-style panel, further immersing the audience in the world of horror comics.

"Creepshow" features five memorable and varied stories:

"Father's Day": A vengeful ghost returns from the grave to seek retribution on Father's Day.

The "Father's Day" segment tells the chilling tale of the Grantham family. Richard Grantham (Warner Shook) and his sister Cass (Elizabeth Regan) go in search of their mother. The segment is known for its iconic line delivered by Nathan's Corpse: "It's Father's Day, Bedelia! I want my cake!"

"Creepshow" was primarily shot on location in Pittsburgh and its suburbs, including Monroeville, where Romero leased an old boys' academy (Penn Hall) to build extensive sets for the film. The "Father's Day" segment, like the rest of the film, showcases Romero's knack for creating atmospheric horror with limited resources.

The segment is also notable for its special effects. The zombie in the "Father's Day" segment has a very grotesque design, with maggots crawling around it, and writhing decaying flesh. This level of detail added a layer of realism to the horror, making the segment all the more terrifying.

"The Lonesome Death of Jordy Verrill": Stephen King stars as a dimwitted farmer who encounters a meteorite that brings disastrous consequences.

"The Lonesome Death of Jordy Verrill" segment tells the chilling tale of Jordy Verrill, a country bumpkin who discovers a meteorite that has landed on his property. After dousing the strange meteorite with water, Jordy's house gets covered with an alien fungus. The segment is known for its iconic line delivered by Jordy Verrill: "Oh, Jordy Verrill, you lunkhead!".

The "The Lonesome Death of Jordy Verrill" segment, like the rest of the film, showcases Romero's knack for creating atmospheric horror with limited resources.

The segment is also notable for its special effects. The alien fungus in the "The Lonesome Death of Jordy Verrill" segment has a very grotesque design, with a glowing green color and a pulsating growth pattern. This level of detail added a layer of realism to the horror, making the segment all the more terrifying.

The "The Lonesome Death of Jordy Verrill" segment, along with the rest of "Creepshow", has left a lasting impact on the horror genre. Its blend of horror and dark comedy, coupled with Romero's distinctive direction and King's sharp writing, has ensured its place as a classic in the annals of horror cinema.

"Something to Tide You Over": A wealthy man exacts a cruel revenge on his wife and her lover, but they return from the dead seeking revenge of their own.

In "Something to Tide You Over", Harry finds himself in a terrifying situation. He discovers a pre-dug hole in the sand only a few feet from the shoreline. Brandishing a handgun, Richard, another character in the story, forces Harry to jump into the hole. He then orders him to begin pulling the sand in, until only his head is sticking out. Richard then sets up a television set, a camera, and a VCR.

"The Crate": A mysterious crate discovered beneath a staircase unleashes a terrifying creature upon an unsuspecting university.

The story revolves around an old wooden crate, marked from an 1834 Arctic expedition, discovered by a janitor beneath the basement stairs at the zoology department of Horlicks University. The crate contains a small yet powerful – and hungry – beast, still alive after 140 years. The creature kills and eats the janitor, as well as Stanley's grad student Charlie Gereson – consuming them entirely, leaving only scraps of clothing behind.

In a twist of fate, English professor Henry Northrup sees the crate-dwelling beast as a way to rid himself of his verbally abusive, alcoholic wife, Wilma. He lures Wilma to the university under the pretense of a distressed female grad student hiding underneath the stairs. As Wilma peers under the stairs, Henry pushes her towards the beast's crate, which promptly devours her.

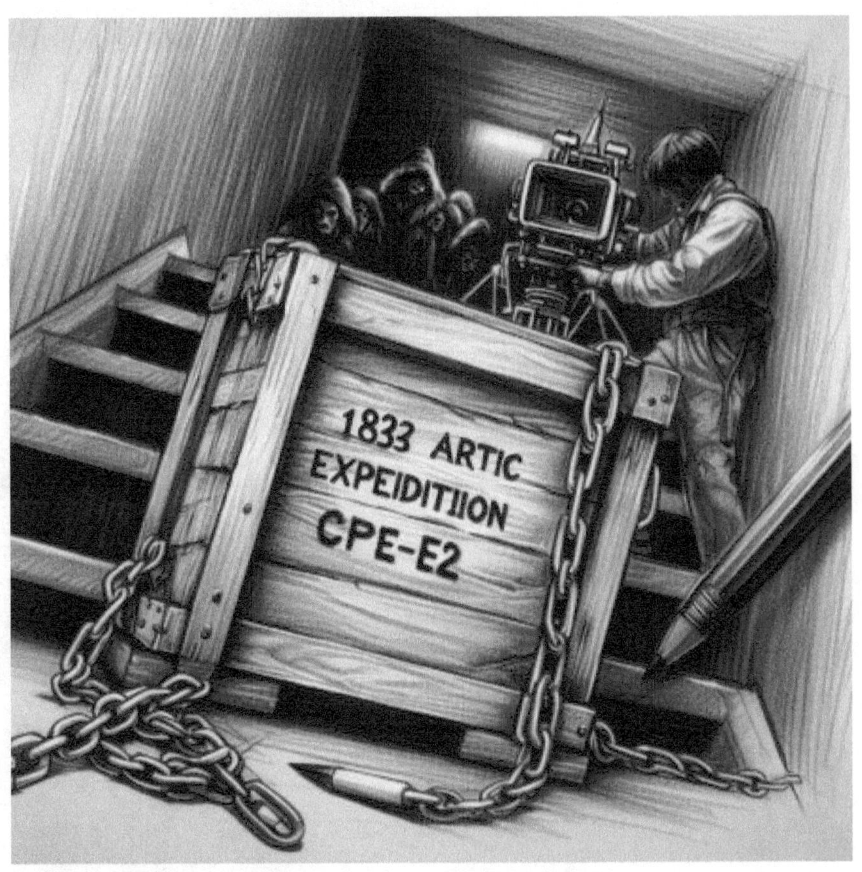

The segment was part of the film "Creepshow," a project that brought together the playful horror fiction of Stephen King with the visual style of George A. Romero. The creature effects were the work of Tom Savini, adding another layer of horror mastery to the segment.

Interestingly, the idea for "Creepshow" came about when Romero and King discovered their shared love for EC Comics. King, who was already a renowned author by then, made his screenwriting debut with "Creepshow," delivering the first draft of the script exactly 60 days after he was asked.

The segment also featured performances by Hal Holbrook as Henry Northrup and Fritz Weaver as Dexter Stanley, bringing the chilling tale to life on the screen.

"The Crate" segment of "Creepshow" is a shining example of the power of collaboration in the horror genre, combining the talents of some of the greatest minds in horror to create a truly unforgettable piece of cinema.

"They're Creeping Up on You!": A ruthless businessman with an extreme fear of bugs finds himself trapped in his sterile apartment with a relentless swarm of cockroaches.

"They're Creeping Up on You" is a chilling vignette featured in the 1982 feature film Creepshow. This segment is the fifth and final story in the movie, not including the framing sequence. The film was directed by George Romero with a screenplay written by Stephen King.

The story revolves around Upson Pratt, a ruthlessly cruel business mogul who suffers from mysophobia, which has rendered him living in a hermetically-sealed penthouse apartment outfitted with electric locks and surveillance cameras. His apparent contacts with the outside world are through the telephone and are primarily made to put-upon employees.

Pratt slowly begins finding cockroaches around his apartment. Being a fanatical insect hater, Pratt arms himself with bug spray in an attempt to combat the insects. The story unfolds as Pratt's fear of insects takes a terrifying turn.

Creepshow was primarily shot on location in Pittsburgh and its suburbs, including Monroeville, where Romero leased an old boys' academy (Penn Hall) to build extensive sets for the film.

"They're Creeping Up on You" has left a lasting impression on viewers, with its blend of horror and dark comedy. The segment, like the rest of the film, is a tribute to the EC horror comics (such as Tales from the Crypt) of the 1950s. It stands as a proclamation to the collaborative genius of George Romero and Stephen King, and remains a memorable part of the horror anthology genre.

Each story in "Creepshow" offers its own unique blend of horror, suspense, and dark humor, keeping audiences engaged and entertained throughout the film.

The 1982 film "Creepshow" is a rich tapestry of horror and comedy, woven together by an ensemble cast of remarkable actors. Each actor, in their unique way, contributed to the anthology's enduring appeal.

Hal Holbrook, a renowned actor, played a significant role in the 1982 film "Creepshow". His performance in the film, particularly as the character Henry Northrup in the segment "The Crate", added depth to the film. Beyond "Creepshow", Holbrook's diverse roles in films like "Julia", "The Fog", "Wall Street", "The Firm", "Hercules", and "Men of Honor" showcase his versatility. His contributions to the film world have left a lasting impact, influencing generations of actors and filmmakers.

Adrienne Barbeau, a distinguished actress, made a significant impact in the film industry with her diverse roles, including her performance in the 1982 film "Creepshow". In the film, she brought to life the character Wilma Northrup in the segment "The Crate", adding a unique dynamic that enhanced the film's overall appeal.

Beyond "Creepshow", Barbeau's filmography is extensive and varied, showcasing her ability to portray a wide range of characters and contribute to the richness of the film world.

In "Creepshow", Barbeau's character, Wilma Northrup, is a pivotal figure in the segment "The Crate". Her performance is key to the success of this segment, which is one of the five short stories that make up the film.

Leslie Nielsen, a celebrated actor, made a significant impact in the film industry with his diverse roles, including his performance in the 1982 film "Creepshow". In the film, he brought to life the character Richard Vickers in the segment "Something To Tide You Over", delivering a performance that was both menacing and gleeful.

Beyond "Creepshow", Nielsen's filmography is extensive and varied, with notable comedic roles in films like "Airplane!" and "The Naked Gun" series. His unique ability to infuse humor and depth into his characters has left a lasting impression on the film industry.

In "Creepshow", Nielsen's character, Richard Vickers, is a pivotal figure in the segment "Something To Tide You Over". His performance is key to the success of this segment, which is one of the five short stories that make up the film.

Carrie Nye, a remarkable actress, left an indelible mark in the film industry with her diverse roles, including her performance in the 1982 film "Creepshow". In the film, she masterfully portrayed the character Sylvia Grantham in the segment "Father's Day", adding a unique dynamic that enhanced the film's overall appeal.

Beyond "Creepshow", Nye's filmography is extensive and varied, with notable roles in films like "The Group", "The Seduction of Joe Tynan", "Too Scared to Scream", and "Hello Again". Her unique ability to infuse depth and complexity into her characters has left a lasting impression on the film industry.

In "Creepshow", Nye's character, Sylvia Grantham, is a pivotal figure in the segment "Father's Day". Her performance is key to the success of this segment, which is one of the five short stories that make up the film.

In conclusion, Carrie Nye's contributions to the film world, particularly through her role in "Creepshow", have left a lasting legacy. Her work in "Creepshow" and other films showcases her talent and versatility, making her a significant figure in film history. Her enduring influence continues to inspire and shape the film world today.

E. G. Marshall, a celebrated actor, left a significant mark on the film industry with his diverse roles, including his performance in the 1982 film "Creepshow". In the film, he masterfully portrayed the character Upson Pratt in the segment "They're Creeping Up on You", delivering a performance that was both memorable and dynamic.

Beyond "Creepshow", Marshall's filmography is extensive and varied, with notable roles in films like "12 Angry Men", "Superman II", and the prime-time drama "Falcon Crest". His unique ability to infuse depth and complexity into his characters has left a lasting impression on the film industry.

Stephen King made a unique contribution to the 1982 film not only as a screenwriter but also as an actor. He portrayed the character Jordy Verrill in the segment "The Lonesome Death of Jordy Verrill", which was based on his own short story "Weeds".

King's portrayal of Jordy, a hapless farmer who undergoes a horrifying transformation after coming into contact with a meteorite, added a touch of authenticity and humor to the film. His performance, though brief, was memorable and endeared him to fans, further cementing his connection to the "Creepshow" universe.

In conclusion, Stephen King's unique dual role in "Creepshow" as both screenwriter and actor has left a lasting imprint on the film world. His work showcases his multifaceted talent and versatility, marking him as a significant figure in film history. His influence continues to inspire and shape the film world today.

Trivia about the "Creepshow"

- "Creepshow" is a unique collaboration that combines Stephen King's twisted imagination with George A. Romero's flair for the macabre.

- Released in 1982, this horror anthology was directed by George A. Romero and written by Stephen King.

- It consists of five supernatural suspense stories, inspired by the old EC horror comic books.

- The movie features well-known actors, including Leslie Nielsen, Hal Holbrook, Adrienne Barbeau, and Ted Danson.

- An alternate ending was scripted but then rewritten for "Something to Tide You Over".

- Leslie Nielsen had a fart machine in his pocket during the shooting.

- Rice Krispies were used as maggots on the corpse's eyes in the first story, "Father's Day".

- "Creepshow" is the only George A. Romero film to open up at number one at the weekend box-office.

- Stephen King was told to play Jordy like Wile E. Coyote.

- Joe Hill, the son of Stephen King, made a cameo as the boy featured in the movie's beginning.

Legacy and Influence

"Creepshow" has gained a significant cult following over the years and is considered a beloved entry in the horror genre. Its successful blend of horror and humor has inspired subsequent anthology films and TV shows, including "Tales from the Darkside: The Movie" and "Trick 'r Treat."

The film's impact on the horror anthology genre is evident in its enduring popularity and the continued appreciation for its homage to horror comics. "Creepshow" remains a testament to George A. Romero's versatility as a filmmaker and his ability to pay homage to the genre while adding his own unique vision.

"Creepshow," continues to captivate audiences even after all these years. It remains a cult classic and holds a special place in the hearts of horror enthusiasts. There are several reasons why this movie still matters and why people continue to connect with it.

Firstly, "Creepshow" is a unique blend of horror and dark humor. It takes inspiration from the classic horror comic books of the 1950s, such as EC Comics. The film is divided into five different segments, each showcasing a different horror story. The narratives are infused with a twisted sense of humor that adds an element of fun to the scares. This combination of horror and humor creates a memorable experience that sets "Creepshow" apart from other horror films of its time.

Additionally, the film boasts an impressive ensemble cast. From Leslie Nielsen to Ted Danson, each actor brings their A-game to their respective segments. Their performances add depth and charisma to the characters, making them more relatable and engaging. Audiences are drawn to these well-portrayed characters, which enhances their overall connection to the film.

Furthermore, the practical effects used in "Creepshow" are a witness to the artistry of the time. In an era before CGI, the movie relied heavily on practical effects, including intricate makeup and prosthetics. The result is a visually stunning display of horror that feels tangible and real. These practical effects have aged exceptionally well, and fans of the film appreciate the craftsmanship involved in bringing the terrifying creatures and gory scenes to life.

Another reason why "Creepshow" continues to resonate with audiences is its anthology format. Each segment tells a self-contained story, offering a diverse range of horror subgenres. From zombies to monsters and supernatural occurrences, the film covers a wide spectrum of terrifying tales. This anthology structure allows viewers to experience a variety of horror scenarios within one film, catering to different preferences and keeping the suspense fresh throughout.

Moreover, "Creepshow" explores universal themes that are still relevant today. The stories delve into topics like revenge, greed, and the consequences of one's actions. Through its horror lens, the film reflects on the darker aspects of human nature, provoking thought and discussion among viewers. It serves as a reminder that our actions can have dire consequences, and that justice and karma are inescapable forces.

The legacy of "Creepshow" is undeniably influential. It has inspired countless filmmakers and artists in the horror genre. Its impact can be seen in other anthology horror films and television series that followed, such as "Tales from the Crypt" and "American Horror Story." The film's success paved the way for future horror anthologies, and its storytelling format continues to be appreciated by both filmmakers and audiences alike.

One of the most compelling aspects of "Creepshow" is the way it taps into our primal fears. The movie delves into the darkest corners of our imagination, bringing to life the monsters that lurk within. It serves as a vessel for our deepest anxieties, allowing us to confront and experience them in a controlled environment. By doing so, "Creepshow" offers a cathartic release, leaving viewers with a sense of relief and empowerment.

The film's visual aesthetics are nothing short of mesmerizing. From the hauntingly beautiful cinematography to the meticulously crafted set designs, "Creepshow" transports its audience to a world where nightmares become reality. The attention to detail is impeccable, immersing viewers in a surreal and atmospheric experience that lingers long after the credits roll.

"Creepshow" also possesses a timeless quality that defies the constraints of its era. While it was released in 1982, the themes it explores are as relevant today as they were then. The film taps into the human condition, exploring our darkest impulses, our deepest secrets, and the consequences of our actions. It serves as a mirror, reflecting back the complexities of our existence and forcing us to confront the darker aspects of ourselves.

Additionally, "Creepshow" has a unique ability to bring people together. It has fostered a community of devoted fans who share a deep appreciation for the film's artistry and storytelling. These fans gather at conventions, host movie nights, and engage in lively discussions about their favorite segments. The film has become a cultural touchstone, creating a sense of camaraderie among those who connect with its macabre charms.

"Creepshow" has achieved a level of cult status that few films can claim. It has permeated popular culture, inspiring countless references, homages, and parodies. Its impact can be felt in the works of other filmmakers, musicians, and artists who have been influenced by its unique blend of horror and humor. "Creepshow" has become an icon, a symbol of the enduring power of storytelling and the human fascination with the unknown.

In conclusion, "Creepshow" matters because it taps into our primal fears, offers a visually stunning experience, explores timeless themes, brings people together, and has achieved a cult status that few films can rival. Its legacy continues to grow, captivating new generations and reminding us of the enduring power of cinema. "Creepshow" is not just a movie; it's an experience that transcends time and leaves an indelible mark on those who dare to venture into its chilling embrace.

Shown for the first time at the Cannes Film Festival on May 16, 1982, and later in the United States on November 12, 1982, "Creepshow" is a cinematic masterpiece directed by George A. Romero and penned by Stephen King. This film marked King's debut as a screenwriter and boasted an ensemble cast.

Distributed by Warner Bros. Pictures, "Creepshow" was made on a budget of $8 million and managed to gross $5,870,889 from 1,127 theaters in its opening weekend, securing the number 1 spot at the U.S. box office. The film eventually collected a total of $21 million at the box office.

The film's journey didn't end there. It found its way into homes through various formats. The "Creepshow" Holiday Specials VHS was available for pre-order starting October 26. The third season of "Creepshow" was released on DVD on December 6, and the fourth season was released on Blu-Ray on December 5, 2023. The original "Creepshow" film is set to be released on Blu-Ray on June 27, 2023.

"Creepshow" lives on in various forms. The original 1982 film was followed by a sequel in 1987. In 2019, an American horror anthology streaming television series titled "Creepshow" was released on Shudder. This series, a continuation of the original film, features multiple episodes with two horror stories per episode. The TV series also includes an animated special titled "A Creepshow Animated Special" and a holiday special titled "A Creepshow Holiday Special".

Each version of "Creepshow" was created to carry forward the legacy of the original film and to bring new horror stories to life in the unique style of the classic E.C. Comics.

Chapter 10: Day of the Dead: The Last Stand of Humanity

In this chapter, we explore George A. Romero's film "Day of the Dead," released in 1985. Serving as the third installment in Romero's original "Dead" series, "Day of the Dead" presents a bleak and intense portrayal of a world on the brink of collapse. This film delves deeper into the themes of societal breakdown, the loss of humanity, and the struggle for survival.

The Setting and Characters

Lori Cardille, a renowned American actress and producer, left an indelible mark on the film world with her performance in the 1985 film "Day of the Dead". Cardille's portrayal of Sarah helped set the stage for future portrayals of strong, fearless women in horror films. Sarah was not just a damsel in distress but a character who was intelligent and in control. This was a significant departure from the traditional depiction of women in horror films.

Interestingly, Romero initially considered Cardille for the role of Mary, the lead scientist. However, he later offered her the part of Sarah, a rebel leader. Eventually, the two characters were merged into one, resulting in a multifaceted female character that challenged traditional gender roles in film.

Cardille's contributions to the film world extend beyond "Day of the Dead". She has had notable roles in the ABC soap opera "The Edge of Night" and "Ryan's Hope". Additionally, she authored a book titled "I'm Gonna Tell: ...an Offbeat Tale of Survival", which recounts her experiences as a survivor of sexual abuse. These diverse roles and experiences have undoubtedly enriched her performances and contributed to her nuanced portrayal of Sarah in "Day of the Dead".

Cardille's contributions to the film world, particularly through her role in "Day of the Dead", are significant. She has redefined the portrayal of women in horror films, bringing strength, intelligence, and complexity to her characters. Her performance as Sarah in "Day of the Dead" remains a landmark in the genre, influencing the depiction of female characters in horror films for years to come.

Terry Alexander, born in Detroit, Michigan, is a celebrated American actor. He is most recognized for his role as John in the 1985 film "Day of the Dead" directed by George A. Romero. The film, part of the

"Night of the Living Dead" series, explores the survival of a group in a zombie apocalypse. Alexander's character, John, plays a crucial role in this narrative.

Alexander's portrayal of John was revolutionary and contributed significantly to the film industry. His unique perspective added depth to the film, cementing its status as a classic in the horror genre.

Beyond "Day of the Dead", Alexander has had a diverse career. He had a regular role on the soap opera "One Life to Live" in the early 1990s, playing police chief Troy Nichols. He has also appeared in numerous films, television shows, and ads, including a notable AIDS PSA.

Terry's contributions to the film world, particularly through his role in "Day of the Dead", are noteworthy. His performance as John has left a lasting impact on the genre and continues to inspire future generations of actors in the film industry.

Joseph Pilato, fondly known as Joe Pilato, was a master of his craft. His portrayal of Captain Rhodes in "Day of the Dead" is a testament to his exceptional talent. The film is a chilling exploration of survival amidst a zombie apocalypse, and Pilato's character, Captain Rhodes, is at the heart of this narrative.

Pilato's performance was nothing short of revolutionary. He breathed life into Captain Rhodes, creating a character that was both relatable and compelling. His unique perspective and nuanced performance added a layer of depth to the film, elevating it from a mere horror flick to a classic in the genre.

As the narrative progresses, we witness Rhodes's descent into madness. He becomes increasingly unstable, aggressive, and violent. Pilato's nuanced performance vividly captures Rhodes's spiraling mental health.

In a climactic scene, a deranged Rhodes confronts the zombie horde. This act of rebellion, leading to his own demise, showcases Pilato's ability to portray the depths of Rhodes's despair and the extent of his mental breakdown.

In essence, Joseph Pilato's portrayal of Captain Rhodes is a compelling exploration of a character's psychological unraveling under extreme circumstances. His performance adds a layer of complexity to the film, making it a classic in the horror genre. His work continues to inspire, setting the stage for future generations of actors in the film industry.

Anthony Dileo Jr.'s portrayal of Private Miguel Salazar in "Day of the Dead" is a riveting journey of a character's transformation. Salazar, initially introduced as a soldier in Colonel Rhodes's troop and Sarah's lover, undergoes a dramatic metamorphosis as the film unfolds.

In the beginning, Salazar is depicted as a soldier trying to navigate the dystopian world overrun by zombies. Dileo Jr. skillfully portrays Salazar's struggle with the grim realities of their situation. However, the relentless exposure to danger and death gradually erodes Salazar's mental stability.

As the narrative progresses, we witness Salazar's descent into madness. He becomes increasingly unstable, aggressive, and violent, especially towards Sarah and his comrades. Dileo Jr.'s nuanced performance vividly captures Salazar's spiraling mental health and suicidal tendencies.

In a climactic scene, a deranged Salazar sabotages the bunker's elevator controls, unleashing the zombie horde into the complex. This act of rebellion, leading to his own demise, showcases Dileo Jr.'s ability to portray the depths of Salazar's despair and the extent of his mental breakdown.

In essence, Anthony Dileo Jr.'s portrayal of Private Miguel Salazar is a compelling exploration of a character's psychological unraveling under extreme circumstances. His performance adds a layer of complexity to the film, making it a classic in the horror genre.

Richard Liberty, an accomplished American film actor, is celebrated for his role as Dr. Matthew "Frankenstein" Logan in George A. Romero's 1985 film "Day of the Dead". The film is a chilling exploration of survival amidst a zombie apocalypse, and Liberty's character, Dr. Logan, is at the heart of this narrative.

Liberty's performance was nothing short of revolutionary. He breathed life into Dr. Logan, creating a character that was both relatable and compelling. His unique perspective and nuanced performance added a layer of depth to the film, elevating it from a mere horror flick to a classic in the genre.

As the narrative progresses, we witness Dr. Logan's descent into madness. He becomes increasingly unstable and obsessed with his work. Liberty's nuanced performance vividly captures Dr. Logan's spiraling mental health.

In a climactic scene, a deranged Dr. Logan confronts the zombie horde. This act of rebellion, leading to his own demise, showcases Liberty's ability to portray the depths of Dr. Logan's despair and the extent of his mental breakdown.

In essence, Richard Liberty's portrayal of Dr. Matthew "Frankenstein" Logan is a compelling exploration of a character's psychological unraveling under extreme circumstances. His performance adds a layer of complexity to the film, making it a classic in the horror genre.

Sherman Howard is renowned for his role as the zombie Bub in George Romero's "Day of the Dead". Howard's portrayal of Bub was nothing short of revolutionary. He breathed life into Bub, creating a character that was both relatable and compelling. His unique perspective and nuanced performance added a layer of depth to the film, elevating it from a mere horror flick to a classic in the genre.

As the narrative progresses, we witness Bub's evolution. Unlike the typical zombies who are driven by their primal instincts, Bub is shown engaging in human-like behavior. Howard's nuanced performance vividly captures Bub's transformation.

In a series of scenes, we see Bub finding pleasure in simple things like leafing through a book, playing with a telephone, and listening to music. This depiction of Bub as a child at heart, finding joy in simple things, adds a layer of depth to the character and the film.

In essence, Sherman Howard's portrayal of Bub in "Day of the Dead" is a compelling exploration of a character's evolution under extreme circumstances. His performance adds a layer of complexity to the film, making it a classic in the horror genre. His work continues to inspire, setting the stage for future generations of actors in the film industry. His legacy is a testament to the power of compelling storytelling and the enduring appeal of well-crafted characters.

Gary Howard Klar is recognized for his role as Private Steel. In the film, set in a world overrun by zombies, Private Steel is a soldier trying to survive in an underground bunker. As the narrative unfolds, we see Steel's character transform. He becomes increasingly unstable and aggressive, a change that Klar skillfully brings to life on screen. His performance adds a layer of complexity to the film, contributing to its status as a classic in the horror genre.

Ralph Marrero delivered a memorable performance as Private Rickles. Set against the backdrop of a zombie apocalypse, Marrero's character, Private Rickles, is a soldier striving to survive in an underground bunker.

Marrero's portrayal of Rickles is a masterclass in character development. As the narrative progresses, Rickles transforms from a soldier to a man on the brink of madness. Marrero's performance captures this transformation with a raw intensity that adds a layer of complexity to the film.

In a world overrun by zombies, Rickles's descent into madness mirrors the chaos and despair of their dystopian reality. Marrero's nuanced performance brings this character to life, making Rickles a character that audiences can't forget.

"Day of the Dead" is set in an underground military bunker where a small group of scientists and soldiers are conducting experiments and research in an attempt to understand and control the zombie epidemic. The film focuses on the deteriorating relationships between the survivors as they face dwindling resources and the constant threat of the undead.

The main characters include Dr. Sarah Bowman, a scientist seeking a solution to the zombie outbreak, Captain Rhodes, a ruthless military leader, and Bub, a zombie who exhibits signs of intelligence and emotion. Through these characters, Romero explores themes of isolation, desperation, and the moral complexities of a world falling apart.

The Loss of Humanity

One of the central themes in "Day of the Dead" is the loss of humanity in the face of extreme circumstances. As the survivors struggle to maintain their sanity and hold on to their humanity, the film questions what it truly means to be human.

The character of Bub, a zombie who shows signs of intelligence, challenges the notion that zombies are mindless monsters. Bub's ability to learn and display emotions raises questions about the nature of humanity and what separates humans from the undead. Romero prompts us to consider whether humanity is defined by physical appearance or by our capacity for empathy and understanding.

"Day of the Dead" delves into the breakdown of societal structures and the conflicts that arise when humanity is pushed to its limits. The tension between the scientists and the military personnel in the bunker mirrors the larger struggles within society.

The scientists, led by Dr. Sarah Bowman, believe in finding a peaceful resolution to the zombie crisis through understanding and research. On the other hand, the military, led by the authoritarian and brutal

Captain Rhodes, resort to violence and aggression as their only means of survival. This clash of ideologies reflects the larger societal conflicts and power struggles that arise in times of crisis.

Practical Effects and Gore

Like Romero's previous "Dead" films, "Day of the Dead" features impressive practical effects and gruesome makeup that contribute to its visceral and realistic depiction of violence and gore. The film's graphic scenes of zombie attacks and dismemberment add to the sense of horror and desperation.

Romero's use of practical effects over CGI gives the film a gritty and tangible quality, immersing the audience in the horrifying world he has created. The practical effects also serve as a validation to Romero's commitment to authenticity and his dedication to pushing the boundaries of the genre.

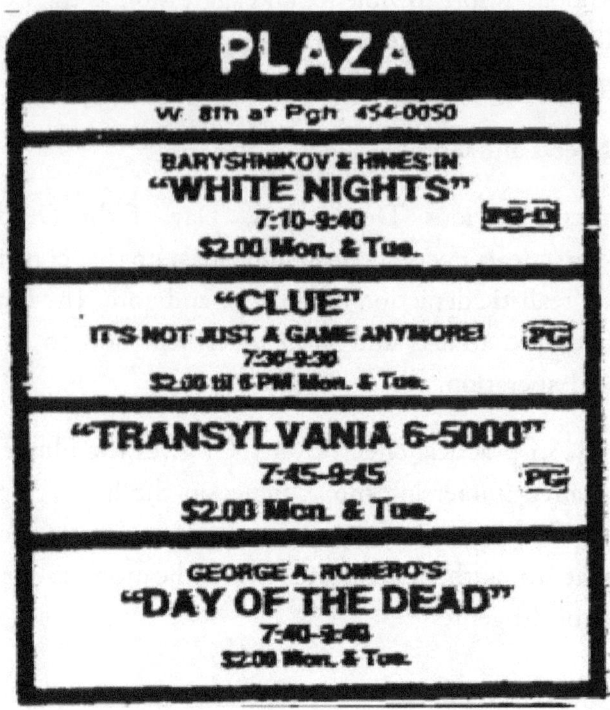

"Day of the Dead" received mixed reviews upon its release but has since gained a cult following and is recognized as a significant entry in Romero's "Dead" series. The film's exploration of the loss of humanity, the breakdown of society, and the moral complexities of survival continue to resonate with audiences.

Trivia from "Day of the Dead" (1985)

- Budget Constraints: The film had a smaller budget compared to its predecessors.

- Underground Setting: The majority of the film takes place in an underground military bunker.

• Zombie Evolution: The concept of zombie evolution is introduced, with signs of intelligence and emotional connections.

• Controversial Release: Initially received mixed reviews and faced controversy due to extreme violence and gore.

• Special Effects: Tom Savini worked on the practical effects, bringing the gory zombie makeup to life.

• Musical Score: The haunting musical score was composed by John Harrison, enhancing the tension and suspense.

• Legacy and Influence: Regarded as one of the most influential zombie films, exploring the human condition in a zombie apocalypse.

• Romero's Vision: Originally envisioned as a larger-scale film with a massive zombie horde.

• Zombie Horde Scene: Achieved through a combination of extras, dummies, and camera angles.

• Alternate Ending: Considered an ending where survivors find an island paradise free from zombies.

Romero's ability to use the zombie genre as a vehicle for social commentary and introspection sets "Day of the Dead" apart. The film serves as a reminder that even in the darkest of times, our humanity and capacity for empathy are what ultimately define us.

Day of the Dead holds a special place in the hearts of horror movie fans around the world. Despite being released over three decades ago, it continues to captivate audiences and remains relevant to this day. This chapter delves into the reasons behind the film's enduring significance and explores what keeps it relevant in the ever-evolving landscape of cinema.

Day of the Dead is an affirmation of George Romero's masterful storytelling and his ability to use horror as a vehicle for social commentary. Set in a post-apocalyptic world overrun by zombies, the film explores themes of human nature, societal breakdown, and the struggle for survival. Romero's narrative draws a parallel between the undead hordes and the decay of humanity, forcing viewers to confront the darker aspects of human behavior.

One of the key elements that make Day of the Dead meaningful to fans is its uncompromising portrayal of human nature under extreme circumstances. The film presents a microcosm of society within an underground military bunker, where tensions run high as survivors grapple with the deteriorating situation. Romero skillfully exposes the fragility of human relationships and the disintegration of social order when faced with a relentless threat. This exploration of human psychology and the erosion of civility continues to resonate with audiences who reflect on their own capacity for both compassion and cruelty.

Another aspect that keeps Day of the Dead relevant is its thought-provoking commentary on authority and power dynamics. Within the bunker, a power struggle emerges between the military and the scientists, each with their own vision for the future of humanity. Romero challenges the notion of absolute authority and questions the lengths individuals are willing to go to maintain control. This examination of power dynamics resonates in a world where authority figures are often scrutinized and questioned.

Furthermore, the film's practical effects and gruesome makeup continue to astound fans. Tom Savini's exceptional work in creating realistic and horrifying zombies has become legendary in the realm of practical effects. Day of the Dead showcases a visceral and grotesque depiction of the undead, leaving an indelible impression on viewers. Even with advancements in CGI, the practical effects in this film remain evidence of the artistry and craftsmanship of the era, attracting fans who appreciate the authenticity and attention to detail.

Day of the Dead's enduring relevance can also be attributed to its exploration of ethical dilemmas in the face of a zombie apocalypse. The film challenges viewers to consider the boundaries of morality and the choices individuals make in desperate situations. The characters grapple with questions of sacrifice, loyalty, and the value of human life. These moral quandaries force audiences to confront their own beliefs and ponder what they would do in similar circumstances.

Moreover, the film's social commentary extends beyond the confines of the zombie genre. Romero uses the undead as a metaphor for the mindless consumerism and conformity that he saw in society. Day of the Dead critiques the dehumanizing effect of mass culture and the loss of individuality. This underlying social critique has remained relevant over the years, as society continues to grapple with issues of conformity and the erosion of personal identity.

The film remains a meaningful and relevant film for fans today due to its exploration of human nature, its commentary on power dynamics and ethics, its exceptional practical effects, and its broader social critique. George Romero's visionary approach to horror continues to captivate audiences, pushing them to contemplate the darker aspects of humanity and the fragility of society. As long as there are horror enthusiasts seeking thought-provoking narratives and social commentary, Day of the Dead will continue to hold its place as a beloved classic in the genre.

Day of the Dead is an absolute gem that has stood the test of time. This masterpiece of horror cinema continues to captivate fans with its chilling tale of a world overrun by zombies. What keeps it relevant? Well, let me tell you, my friend.

First of all, the sheer brilliance of George Romero's storytelling is what makes this film so meaningful to fans today. He takes us on a journey into a post-apocalyptic world where the dead walk the Earth, and humanity is on the brink of extinction. But it's not just about the zombies; it's about the human characters and their struggle for survival. Romero presents us with a diverse cast of characters, each with their own strengths, weaknesses, and hidden agendas. It's this depth of characterization that keeps viewers engaged and invested in their fate.

But let's not forget the gore! Tom Savini's incredible special effects work in Day of the Dead is a sight to behold. The zombies in this film are some of the most realistic and gruesome ever put on screen. Savini's attention to detail is simply unmatched, and his work continues to impress even in today's era of CGI. Fans of practical effects will always appreciate the artistry and craftsmanship that went into creating the chilling undead in this film.

And then there's the social commentary. Romero was known for using his zombie films as a vehicle to critique society, and Day of the Dead is no exception. It explores themes of power, authority, and the breakdown of social order. Within the confines of a military bunker, we witness the clash between the military personnel and the scientists, each vying for control and dominance. This power struggle serves as a metaphor for the struggles we face in our own lives and the corrupting influence of power.

Lastly, let's talk about the sheer entertainment value of Day of the Dead. It's a rollercoaster ride of suspense, horror, and unexpected twists. The tension builds throughout the film, keeping viewers on the edge of their seats. And let's not forget the iconic climax, where all hell breaks loose and the zombies take center stage. It's a thrilling and satisfying conclusion that leaves fans craving for more.

In summary, Day of the Dead is a timeless classic that continues to resonate with fans today. Its compelling storytelling, jaw-dropping practical effects, thought-provoking social commentary, and sheer entertainment value are what keep it relevant in the hearts and minds of horror enthusiasts. So, if you haven't experienced the terror of Day of the Dead, I highly recommend you grab some popcorn, turn off the lights, and prepare for a chilling journey into the world of the undead. You won't be disappointed!

In the summer of 1985, a cinematic phenomenon was unleashed upon the world. George A. Romero's "Day of the Dead", the third installment in his iconic zombie horror series, made its debut. The film first saw the light of day in Hicksville, New York on June 30, before being released nationwide on July 19. The United Film Distribution Company (UFDC) was responsible for bringing this chilling tale to theaters.

Despite a modest budget of around $4 million, the film managed to rake in an impressive $34 million at the global box office. Although it didn't immediately achieve the acclaim of its predecessors, "Day of the Dead" has since risen from the ashes to become a beloved cult classic, even earning the distinction of being Romero's personal favorite in the original Dead trilogy.

The film's journey didn't end with its theatrical run. In 1989, it clawed its way into homes with a VHS release. The undead saga continued to spread with a DVD release in 2013, and a Blu-ray release in 2007. Each new format brought with it a new version of the film, complete with additional scenes, commentary tracks, and special features.

The existence of these multiple versions of the script can be traced back to Romero's decision to make the film on a lower budget and release it unrated as part of a three-film deal with UFDC. This choice resulted in a variety of unique elements being included in each version. Over the years, "Day of the Dead" has continued to infect new generations of fans, its enduring popularity ensuring its release in various formats.

Chapter 11: Monkey Shines: An Experiment in Fear

Romero's Psychological Thriller

In 1988, George A. Romero ventured into the realm of psychological horror with his film "Monkey Shines." Departing from the supernatural and societal commentary that defined much of his previous work, Romero delved into the complex world of human psychology, exploring themes of dependency, control, and the darker side of human nature.

The Story Unleashed

"Monkey Shines" centers around Allan Mann, a former athlete who becomes paralyzed after a tragic accident. Feeling isolated and trapped, Allan is introduced to Ella, a highly intelligent capuchin monkey trained to assist him. Initially, Ella brings joy and companionship to Allan's life, but their relationship takes a sinister turn as the monkey's behavior becomes increasingly aggressive and uncontrollable.

A Study of Human Nature

Beneath the surface of "Monkey Shines" lies a deep exploration of the human psyche. The film delves into themes of dependency, power dynamics, and the lengths to which one will go to assert control over others. Romero uses the monkey as a metaphor for the darker aspects of human nature, as Ella's actions mirror the suppressed desires and impulses within Allan himself.

The Psychological Thrills

"Monkey Shines" is a slow-burning psychological thriller that gradually builds tension and suspense. Romero masterfully creates an atmosphere of unease and paranoia, as the audience is left questioning the true nature of the relationship between Allan and Ella. The film's psychological twists and turns keep viewers on the edge of their seats, exploring the fine line between sanity and madness.

Critically Acclaimed Performances

The performances in "Monkey Shines" are a testament to the film's success. Jason Beghe delivers a compelling portrayal of Allan, capturing the character's vulnerability and descent into obsession. However, it is the performance of Boo, the capuchin monkey who plays Ella, that steals the show. Boo's ability to convey a range of emotions and unnerving behavior adds an extra layer of intensity to the film.

Monkey Shines is a 1988 film directed by George A. Romero that boasts a remarkable ensemble of actors. Each actor brought their unique talent and charisma to the film, making it a memorable piece of cinema.

Jason Beghe, a seasoned actor with a career that spans over three decades, has left an indelible mark on the film industry. His role in the 1988 film "Monkey Shines," is particularly noteworthy.

In "Monkey Shines," Beghe masterfully portrays Allan Mann, a young athlete turned quadriplegic. This role was a turning point in Beghe's career, demonstrating his ability to bring complex characters to life. His performance was met with universal acclaim.

Allan Mann, a law student and athlete, becomes quadriplegic after a truck accident. As he grapples with his new reality, he forms a bond with Ella, an intelligent service monkey. However, Ella turns homicidal after being injected with an experimental serum of human brain tissue. This unique plotline explores the human-animal relationship, and Beghe's performance adds depth to this exploration.

Beghe's portrayal of Allan Mann stands out for its emotional depth. Allan is not only grappling with the physical challenges of his condition but also the emotional and psychological toll it takes. His girlfriend leaves him, and he attempts suicide but fails. These experiences add layers to Allan's character, and Beghe navigates these layers with skill and sensitivity.

Beyond "Monkey Shines," Beghe has made significant contributions to the film world through a variety of roles. He has appeared in popular television shows such as "Chicago P.D.," "CSI: NY," and "Californication," and in films such as "Thelma & Louise," "G.I. Jane," and "X-Men: First Class". His diverse roles demonstrate his versatility as an actor and his ability to bring depth and complexity to different characters.

In addition to his acting career, Beghe is also a talented voice actor. He has lent his voice to characters in video games such as "Call of Duty: Modern Warfare 3" and "The Bureau: XCOM Declassified". This work further showcases his versatility and talent.

Beghe's portrayal of Allan Mann in "Monkey Shines" and his contributions to the film world more broadly demonstrate his talent, versatility, and dedication to his craft. His performances captivate audiences and bring depth and complexity to a range of characters. His work in "Monkey Shines" and beyond has left a significant impact on the film industry.

John Pankow, a versatile actor, has left a significant imprint on the film industry. His memorable performance in the 1988 film "Monkey Shines," where he played Geoffrey, is particularly noteworthy. In "Monkey Shines," Pankow brings to life the character of Geoffrey, a scientist who inadvertently turns a monkey into a killer. This compelling portrayal adds a unique dynamic to the film.

Beyond "Monkey Shines," Pankow has made his mark in the film world through a variety of roles. Starting his career on-stage in New York, he has appeared in numerous Off-Broadway and Broadway plays. He has also worked with some of the industry's most respected directors, showcasing his versatility and ability to bring complex characters to life.

In addition to his film and stage career, Pankow has made guest appearances on numerous popular television series. His portrayal of Ira Buchman on the hit sitcom "Mad About You," showcased his comedic timing and acting skills to a wide audience.

Pankow's performances in supporting roles have left a lasting impact on audiences. His presence in films from the iconic war film "Platoon" to the cult classic "To Live and Die in L.A.," adds depth and authenticity to the stories being told.

In conclusion, John Pankow's contributions to the film world, from his portrayal of Geoffrey in "Monkey Shines" to his diverse roles in film and television, demonstrate his talent, versatility, and dedication to his craft. His performances captivate audiences, bringing depth and complexity to a range of characters. His work has left a significant impact on the film industry.

Kate McNeil, an accomplished American actress, has left her mark on the film industry. Her performance in the 1988 film "Monkey Shines," where she played the role of Melanie Parker, is particularly memorable.

In "Monkey Shines," McNeil brings to life the character of Melanie Parker, a specialist in quadriplegia and helper monkeys. Her character forms a romantic relationship with Allan Mann, the film's protagonist. The film notably includes an intimate love scene with a severely handicapped protagonist. McNeil's portrayal of Melanie Parker adds a unique dynamic to the film, showcasing her ability to bring depth and complexity to her characters.

Beyond "Monkey Shines," McNeil has made her mark in the film world through a variety of roles. She kick started her acting career on the soap opera "As the World Turns" in 1981. In 1983, she landed the leading role in the slasher film "The House on Sorority Row". She has also appeared in numerous popular television series, adding depth and authenticity to the stories being told.

Joyce Van Patten, a seasoned American actress, has left a significant imprint on the film industry. Her performance in the 1988 film "Monkey Shines," where she played Dorothy, Allan Mann's overbearing mother, is particularly memorable.

In "Monkey Shines," Van Patten's character Dorothy is a domineering and selfish woman who moves in to care for Allan, her quadriplegic son. Her overbearing nature further complicates Allan's struggle to adjust to his new life. Van Patten's portrayal of Dorothy adds a unique dynamic to the film, showcasing her ability to bring depth and complexity to her characters.

Christine Forrest, an accomplished actress and producer, has left a significant mark on the film industry. Her memorable role as the nurse in the 1988 film "Monkey Shines" is particularly noteworthy.

In "Monkey Shines," Forrest's character is an insufferable nurse. She is a classic harridan, a term used to describe a strict, bossy, or belligerent old woman. Her character adds a unique dynamic to the film, showcasing her ability to bring depth and complexity to her characters.

Beyond "Monkey Shines," Forrest has made her mark in the film world through a variety of roles. She is the former wife of George A. Romero and appeared in many of his films. Forrest met Romero on the set of "Season of the Witch" and went on to appear in "Martin," "Knightriders," "Two Evil Eyes," and "The Dark Half," which she also co-produced. In addition to appearing in a small role in the film, she was a producer and assistant director on "Dawn of the Dead".

Rounding out the cast. Stephen Root and Stanley Tucci, both luminaries in the film industry, have left an indelible mark with their diverse roles. Their performances in the 1988 film "Monkey Shines" are particularly striking.

Stephen Root, in "Monkey Shines," breathed life into the character of Dean Burbage, adding a unique dynamic to the film. Beyond this role, Root's career is studded with a variety of roles that showcase his versatility. From his debut in "Crocodile Dundee II" to his cameo in "Ghost," Root's performances have consistently captivated audiences.

Stanley Tucci, on the other hand, portrayed Dr. John Wiseman in "Monkey Shines," an arrogant surgeon responsible for the protagonist's debilitating state. Tucci's portrayal added depth to the film, showcasing his ability to bring complexity to his characters. Beyond "Monkey Shines," Tucci's filmography is equally impressive, with roles in films like "Prizzi's Honor," "Deconstructing Harry," "Road to Perdition," and "The Terminal." His directorial debut with "Big Night" further showcases his talent and versatility.

Each actor's unique talent and charisma contributed to the success of Monkey Shines, making it a classic in the annals of cinema.

Here are some interesting trivia about "Monkey Shines":

• First Studio Film: "Monkey Shines" was the first studio film for George A. Romero. However, the studio he was working with, Orion Pictures, had re-cut the film against Romero's wishes which contributed to the box office failure of the film.

• Explicit Scene: This film was one of the very few films depicting a quadriplegic having sex. Producer Charles Evans said the oral sex scene between Kate McNeil and Jason Beghe was much more explicit as originally shot.

• Budget and Box Office: The film marked Romero's first major studio feature, and was his second-most expensive film at that time, with a budget of $7 million. Despite the high budget, the film received a lackluster box-office reception, grossing $5.3 million against its $7 million budget.

• Setting: The film's setting was changed from Oxford, England, where the novel was set, to Pittsburgh, Pennsylvania, a city in which Romero had long resided and often set his films.

● Post-production: The film had a protracted post-production and editing process, as Romero shot more film than he had on any of his previous projects, particularly due to the use of live monkeys.

● Based on a Novel: "Monkey Shines" was based on the 1983 British novel of the same title by Michael Stewart. It follows a young athlete who becomes a paralyzed quadriplegic and develops a bond with an intelligent service monkey named "Ella" who becomes homicidal after she is injected with an experimental serum of human brain tissue.

● First Film Role: This was the first film role for Stephen Root, then a stage actor. According to Root, he had been instructed by his agent not to let the casting directors know that he was inexperienced with film as an actor.

Legacy and Impact

While "Monkey Shines" may not have achieved the same level of commercial success as some of Romero's other works, it remains a notable entry in his filmography. The film showcases Romero's ability to transcend genres and tackle the complexities of the human psyche. "Monkey Shines" serves as a reminder that the true horrors can often be found within ourselves.

Monkey Shines is a film that continues to captivate and resonate with fans even after more than three decades since its release in 1988. This psychological horror thriller explores themes of dependency, human nature, and the blurred lines between man and animal. Despite its age, Monkey Shines remains a thought-provoking and unsettling cinematic experience that continues to find relevance in the hearts of its fans.

At its core, Monkey Shines delves into the depths of human vulnerability and the consequences of tampering with nature. The story follows Allan Mann, a former athlete who becomes quadriplegic after a tragic accident. As Allan's world crumbles around him, he finds solace and companionship in the form of Ella, a highly intelligent capuchin monkey trained to assist him. However, what begins as a seemingly innocent bond between man and animal soon spirals into a nightmarish tale of obsession and psychological terror.

One of the reasons Monkey Shines retains its significance is its exploration of the human-animal relationship. The film challenges our perceptions of animals as mere companions or pets. Ella, the monkey, is more than just a sidekick in the narrative; she becomes a metaphor for the primal instincts and dark desires lurking within the human psyche. Romero cleverly blurs the lines between human and animal, forcing viewers to question their own capacity for both love and destruction.

Furthermore, Monkey Shines tackles the theme of dependency and the lengths we go to find solace in others. Allan's paralysis leaves him emotionally and physically vulnerable, and his reliance on Ella intensifies as the story progresses. The film examines the intricate dynamics of dependency and the dangers that can arise when one becomes too reliant on another for their well-being. This exploration of human vulnerability strikes a chord with audiences, reminding us of the delicate balance between trust and control in our own lives.

Monkey Shines also delves into the concept of scientific experimentation and the ethical dilemmas it poses. Allan's friend and scientist, Geoffrey Fisher, performs secret experiments on Ella, which inadvertently enhance her intelligence and emotional connection to Allan. This subplot raises questions about the boundaries of scientific progress and the moral implications of manipulating nature. As society grapples with advancements in technology and genetic engineering, Monkey Shines serves as a cautionary tale, reminding us of the potential consequences when we play god.

Moreover, Monkey Shines is still relevant today due to its exploration of the darker aspects of human nature. The film pushes the boundaries of psychological horror, delving into the depths of our subconscious fears and desires. It forces us to confront our own inner demons and contemplate the darkness that lurks within each of us. In an age where horror films often rely on cheap jump scares and gore, Monkey Shines stands out as a masterclass in psychological terror, leaving a lasting impact on its viewers.

Despite being a product of the late 80s, Monkey Shines retains its relevance through its timeless themes and expert storytelling. George Romero's skillful direction, combined with strong performances and a haunting score, creates an atmosphere of dread that continues to resonate with audiences today. The film's exploration of the human-animal relationship, dependency, ethical dilemmas, and the darker aspects of human nature ensures its place as a cult classic that stands the test of time.

Monkey Shines: A Profound Journey into the Depths of Fear

Monkey Shines, directed by the masterful George Romero, is an absolute tour de force that continues to captivate fans with its gripping narrative and thought-provoking themes. Released in 1988, this psychological horror gem has managed to transcend time and retain its meaningfulness in the hearts of its devoted followers.

The film's enduring significance lies in its exploration of the primal fears that reside within the human psyche. Monkey Shines taps into the darkest recesses of our minds, delving into themes of isolation, dependency, and the loss of control. By taking us on a journey through the mind of Allan Mann, a once-able-bodied man who becomes quadriplegic, the film forces us to confront our deepest fears and question our own vulnerabilities.

Monkey Shines challenges the traditional human-animal relationship, pushing the boundaries of what we perceive as companionship. Ella, the highly intelligent capuchin monkey, becomes a symbol of the untamed forces that reside within us all. She represents the raw instincts we often suppress, reminding us that we are not as far removed from our animalistic nature as we may think. Romero's skillful storytelling blurs the lines between man and beast, leaving a lasting impression on viewers.

Another aspect that keeps Monkey Shines relevant is its exploration of the complex dynamics of dependency. Allan's paralysis leaves him emotionally and physically vulnerable, and his bond with Ella becomes his lifeline. Through their relationship, the film delves into the intricate web of human dependency, highlighting the dangers that arise when one person becomes too reliant on another. This theme strikes a chord with audiences, as we grapple with our own desires for connection and the fear of losing control.

Monkey Shines also poses thought-provoking questions about the limits of scientific experimentation and the moral implications of tampering with nature. As Allan's friend, Geoffrey Fisher, conducts secret experiments on Ella, the film challenges us to consider the ethical boundaries of scientific progress. In an age where technology and genetic engineering continue to advance, Monkey Shines serves as a cautionary tale, reminding us of the potential consequences when we overstep your bounds.

Monkey Shines delves into the depths of our subconscious fears and desires, forcing us to confront the darkness that resides within us all. Romero's expert direction and eerie atmosphere create a sense of dread that lingers long after the credits roll. In a genre often saturated with superficial scares, Monkey Shines stands as a testimony to the power of psychological horror.

In conclusion, Monkey Shines is a timeless masterpiece that continues to captivate fans with its profound exploration of fear, dependency, and the blurred lines between man and animal. George Romero's visionary direction, combined with strong performances and a chilling score, ensures that the film remains a relevant and thought-provoking piece of cinema. Monkey Shines serves as a powerful reminder that our deepest fears and vulnerabilities are universal, transcending time and resonating with audiences for years to come.

"Monkey Shines", a chilling blend of science fiction and psychological horror, was unveiled to the world on July 29th. The film, distributed by Orion Pictures, was a daring venture that unfortunately didn't quite hit its mark at the box office, earning $5.3 million against its $7 million budget.

As the years passed, "Monkey Shines" found new life in various formats. While the exact release date of the VHS version remains elusive, the DVD version made its debut on March 7, 2000. The film also found its way into the Blu-Ray realm, with one version released on November 18, 2014, and a special Collector's Edition by Umbrella Entertainment hitting the shelves in December 2023.

Chapter 12: Two Evil Eyes

Romero's Collaboration with Dario Argento

In 1990, George A. Romero teamed up with Italian horror maestro Dario Argento to create the anthology film "Two Evil Eyes." Inspired by the works of Edgar Allan Poe, the film is a collection of two separate stories, each directed by Romero and Argento respectively. This unique collaboration brought together two iconic directors and resulted in a chilling exploration of human darkness and the macabre.

The Stories Unveiled

"Two Evil Eyes" consists of two distinct segments: "The Facts in the Case of Mr. Valdemar" directed by Romero, and "The Black Cat" directed by Argento. Each segment presents a different Poe-inspired tale of horror and delves into the depths of the human psyche.

Romero's "The Facts in the Case of Mr. Valdemar"

In Romero's segment, "The Facts in the Case of Mr. Valdemar," the story follows a dying man named Mr. Valdemar who is experimented upon by a sinister hypnotist. As the hypnotist tries to extend Valdemar's life, eerie and supernatural events unfold, blurring the line between life and death.

Argento's "The Black Cat"

In Argento's segment, "The Black Cat," the story centers around a crime photographer who becomes obsessed with photographing death. His obsession leads him down a dark path, as he becomes entangled in a web of murder and supernatural vengeance.

The Collaboration of Maestros

"Two Evil Eyes" showcases the unique styles of both Romero and Argento. Romero's segment reflects his trademark social commentary and exploration of human morality, while Argento's segment embodies his visual flair and penchant for suspenseful and gruesome storytelling.

The collaboration between these two horror maestros resulted in a film that blends their distinct sensibilities while paying homage to the master of horror, Edgar Allan Poe.

Adrienne Barbeau delivers a compelling performance as Jessica Valdemar. Her character, a flight attendant turned trophy wife, schemes to inherit her dying husband's fortune. While the role could have easily fallen into cliché, Barbeau brings a depth of sympathy to Jessica that is unexpected.

Barbeau's contributions to the film world extend beyond "Two Evil Eyes". She first gained recognition in the 1970s, starring in Broadway's "Grease" and the sitcom "Maude". In the 1980s, she began appearing in horror and science fiction films, including "The Fog", "Escape from New York", "Creepshow", and "Swamp Thing". She also lent her voice to Catwoman in the DC Animated Universe.

Barbeau's dedication to her craft is evident in her diverse roles and her commitment to both mainstream and independent cinema. She has starred in over 25 theatrical productions and continues to captivate audiences with her intense and authentic performances. Her recent work includes projects for Amazon Prime, Warner Bros, a new video game, and her fifth book "Grease Tell Me More, Tell Me More".

In "Two Evil Eyes", Ramy Zada's character, Dr. Hoffman, is entangled in a plot with his lover, Jessica Valdemar, to swindle her dying husband's wealth. Despite some critics pointing out inconsistencies in his performance, Zada's role added a layer of suspense and intrigue to the film.

Beyond "Two Evil Eyes", Zada has demonstrated his acting prowess in numerous films and TV. His role as Judge Nicholas Marshall in CBS's "Dark Justice", the first network TV series shot in Barcelona, Spain, further established his reputation.

Zada's creative pursuits include screenwriting, directing, voice-over acting, and even creating/hosting a food reality TV show, "America's Happy Hour". These endeavors highlight his creativity and versatility, further cementing his place in the film world.

In summary, Ramy Zada's diverse roles, including his portrayal of Dr. Robert Hoffman in "Two Evil Eyes", and his various contributions to the film world, underscore his significant impact on the industry. His enduring appeal to audiences attests to the resonance of his performances and contributions.

Bingo O'Malley and E. G. Marshall brought the characters of Ernest Valdemar and Steven Pike to life, respectively.

Bingo O'Malley, often hailed as "Pittsburgh's finest actor", portrayed Ernest Valdemar, a wealthy man on his deathbed. His performance added a layer of depth to the film's narrative.

E. G. Marshall took on the role of Steven Pike, a lawyer who grows suspicious of Jessica, Valdemar's wife. His portrayal added an element of intrigue to the plot.

The performances of both actors were pivotal to the film's success. Their nuanced portrayals of their respective characters enriched the film's intricate plotlines, heightening its suspense and intrigue.

Harvey Keitel's performance in the 1990 film "Two Evil Eyes" is incredible. In the film, he plays Roderick Usher, an artist with a morbid fascination for crime scenes and gory dismemberments. His character is complex and tormented, particularly by his girlfriend's new black cat.

Keitel's portrayal of Usher showcases his ability to bring depth and complexity to his characters. His performances are often marked by their intensity and authenticity, making him a powerful presence on screen. This is evident in his role in "Two Evil Eyes", where he manages to convey a sense of inner turmoil and conflict.

Beyond "Two Evil Eyes", Keitel has made significant contributions to the film world. He has collaborated with renowned filmmakers like Martin Scorsese, Quentin Tarantino, and Ridley Scott, delivering memorable performances in films like "Mean Streets", "Taxi Driver", "Reservoir Dogs", and "Pulp Fiction".

Keitel's commitment to independent cinema is also noteworthy. He has consistently chosen to work with emerging directors and take on challenging roles in unconventional films. This dedication has not only showcased his range as an actor but has also significantly contributed to the growth and success of independent cinema.

John Amos, a celebrated actor recognized for his diverse roles, made a significant contribution to the film as Detective Legrand. Detective Legrand is a key figure in "The Black Cat", a segment of the film inspired by Poe's story. This part of the film delves into chilling crime scenes, enhancing the narrative's suspense and horror.

Amos's depiction of Detective Legrand deepened the film's narrative and heightened its eerie atmosphere. His performance showcases his acting versatility and his knack for embodying complex characters.

Madeleine Potter and Sally Kirkland play Annabel and Eleonora respectively. Their performances add a touch of elegance and mystery to the segment.

Each actor, with their unique style and talent, contributes to the overall allure of "Two Evil Eyes", making it a memorable piece in George A. Romero's filmography.

Trivia about "Two Evil Eyes"

- Dario Argento, one of the directors, originally wanted the film to be a collaboration between four directors: him, George A. Romero, John Carpenter, and Wes Craven.

- The film was initially intended to be an anthology film consisting of four segments based on Edgar Allan Poe stories, each by a different director.

- "Two Evil Eyes" consists of adaptations of two separate Edgar Allan Poe stories, "The Facts in the Case of M. Valdemar" and "The Black Cat".

- The segment "The Black Cat" is notable for containing over 100 cuts.

- The makeup effects for the film were provided by Tom Savini.

"Two Evil Eyes" received mixed reviews upon its release, with some praising the collaboration and the individual segments, while others felt that the film lacked cohesion. Despite its mixed reception, "Two Evil Eyes" remains an intriguing entry in both Romero's and Argento's filmographies. It stands as a testament to their creativity and ability to craft atmospheric and chilling tales of horror.

While "Two Evil Eyes" may not be as well-known as some of Romero's or Argento's other works, it serves as a reminder of the enduring influence of Edgar Allan Poe on the horror genre. The film showcases the timeless nature of Poe's stories and the ability of talented directors to bring them to life on the silver screen.

"Two Evil Eyes," continues to captivate and resonate with fans even today. As we delve into the reasons behind its enduring significance, we uncover the elements that have kept it relevant and firmly embedded in the hearts of horror enthusiasts.

One of the reasons why "Two Evil Eyes" continues to resonate is its unwavering commitment to the spirit of Poe's original works. Romero's screenplay remains faithful to the essence of Poe's stories, while also injecting his own unique brand of horror. The film pays homage to the gothic atmosphere and psychological torment that Poe was renowned for, all while adding a modern twist that appeals to contemporary audiences.

Furthermore, the film boasts an impressive ensemble cast, with notable performances by Adrienne Barbeau, E.G. Marshall, and Harvey Keitel. These talented actors bring depth and authenticity to their roles, elevating the film beyond mere horror tropes. Their nuanced portrayals add a layer of realism to the characters, making their experiences and struggles all the more relatable.

In addition to the film's stellar cast, the visual aesthetics of "Two Evil Eyes" play a crucial role in its continued relevance. Romero's mastery of cinematography and practical effects shines through, creating an atmosphere that is both visually stunning and hauntingly atmospheric. From the dimly lit corridors of Mr. Valdemar's mansion to the claustrophobic confines of the basement in "The Black Cat," Romero's visual storytelling keeps viewers on the edge of their seats, immersed in a world of terror.

Moreover, the themes explored in "Two Evil Eyes" remain as pertinent today as they were when the film was first released. The examination of mortality, the consequences of unchecked obsessions, and the blurred lines between sanity and madness continue to strike a chord with audiences. Romero's ability to tap into these universal fears and anxieties is a proclamation to his filmmaking prowess and his understanding of what truly terrifies us.

The enduring appeal of "Two Evil Eyes" lies in its ability to evoke a sense of nostalgia among horror enthusiasts. Released during a period when the horror genre was undergoing a renaissance, the film represents a bridge between the classic works of horror auteurs like Romero and the emerging wave of modern horror. It serves as a reminder of the genre's rich history while embracing the evolving landscape of horror cinema.

"Two Evil Eyes" remains a meaningful and relevant film for fans of the horror genre. Its commitment to Poe's original works, its exceptional cast, its visually striking aesthetics, and its exploration of timeless themes all contribute to its enduring appeal. As we continue to celebrate the legacy of George Romero, "Two Evil Eyes" stands as a recognition of his visionary storytelling and his ability to create horror experiences that transcend time."

"Two Evil Eyes," has left an indelible mark on horror fans, and it's no wonder why. This gruesome masterpiece lures viewers into a realm of darkness and terror, where the twisted genius of Edgar Allan Poe meets the visionary brilliance of Romero.

The first segment, "The Facts in the Case of Mr. Valdemar," thrusts us into a macabre experiment where a dying man clings desperately to life. It's a chilling exploration of the boundaries between life and death, showcasing Romero's ability to tap into our deepest fears. And let's not forget the jaw-dropping practical effects that will leave you questioning reality.

As if that's not enough, "Two Evil Eyes" slams us into the depraved world of "The Black Cat." This segment delves into the sinister mind of a man consumed by guilt and obsession. Harvey Keitel's portrayal of a tormented artist is nothing short of mesmerizing, and the climax... well, let's just say it will haunt your nightmares long after the credits roll.

But what truly sets "Two Evil Eyes" apart is its unapologetic embrace of gore and violence. Romero delivers gruesome scenes that push the boundaries of what we consider acceptable. From blood-soaked rooms to the brutal disintegration of a human body, this film leaves no stone unturned in its quest to shock and disturb.

And let's not forget the iconic performances by Adrienne Barbeau and E.G. Marshall. Barbeau's portrayal of a cunning seductress is as mesmerizing as it is terrifying, while Marshall's commanding presence adds an extra layer of intensity to the film. Their chemistry on-screen is palpable, adding a dynamic dimension to the already gripping narrative.

"Two Evil Eyes" has stood the test of time because it refuses to conform to the limitations of the horror genre. It dares to push boundaries, both visually and thematically, leaving audiences on the edge of their seats and craving more. It's a testament to Romero's audacious vision and his ability to create a film that resonates with horror enthusiasts across generations.

So, if you're ready to dive headfirst into a world of darkness, where the line between the living and the dead blurs, "Two Evil Eyes" is waiting. Brace yourself for a cinematic experience that will leave you gasping for breath, questioning your own sanity, and craving more of Romero's twisted genius. This film is not for the faint of heart, but for those brave enough to confront their deepest fears, it's an unforgettable journey into the depths of horror.

The film first saw the light of day in Italy on January 25, 1990, before making its way to American shores on October 25, 1991. Distributed by Artisti Associati International and Taurus Entertainment Company in Italy and the United States respectively, the film, despite its modest box office earnings of $349,618, left an indelible mark on the genre.

As the years rolled by, "Two Evil Eyes" found its way into the homes of horror aficionados worldwide. The DVD release on April 29, 2003, allowed fans to relive the terror in the comfort of their living rooms. The advent of Blu-Ray technology saw the film being released in this format on October 29, 2019, followed by a 4K Ultra HD + Special Features Blu-ray on August 24, 2021, offering viewers an even more immersive experience.

Chapter 13: The Dark Half: Serious writer or serial killer.

Romero's Adaptation of Stephen King's Novel

In 1993, George A. Romero took on the task of adapting Stephen King's novel "The Dark Half" into a feature film. Known for his mastery of the horror genre, Romero brought his unique vision to this psychological thriller that explores the duality of human nature, the power of imagination, and the consequences of hidden secrets.

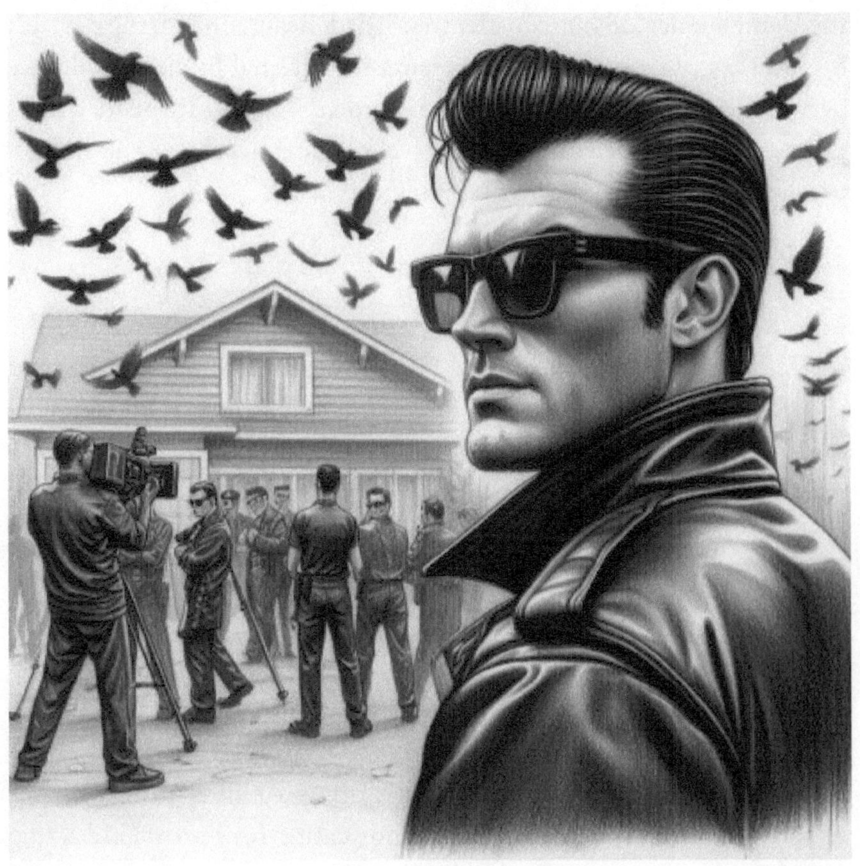

The Story Unveiled

"The Dark Half" follows the life of Thad Beaumont, a successful author who is forced to confront a dark secret from his past. Thad discovers that his alter ego, George Stark, a pseudonym under which he wrote violent and gritty novels, has come to life and is committing a series of gruesome murders. As Thad struggles to distance himself from his alter ego, he becomes embroiled in a battle between reality and fiction.

Duality and Identity

At the heart of "The Dark Half" is the exploration of duality and the complexities of human identity. Thad Beaumont's struggle with his alter ego, George Stark, represents the internal battles we all face between our public personas and hidden desires. Through Thad's journey, Romero delves into the psychological depths of the human psyche and questions the nature of identity itself.

The Power of Imagination

"The Dark Half" also delves into the power of imagination and the blurred lines between reality and fiction. Thad's ability to create vivid and compelling stories becomes both a gift and a curse as his creations manifest in the real world. Romero skillfully captures the dark and twisted nature of King's novel, emphasizing the transformative power of the written word and the dangers of unchecked creativity.

In the realm of horror and suspense, few films have left as indelible a mark as George A. Romero's 1993 masterpiece, "The Dark Half". The film's success can be attributed to its talented cast, each of whom brought their unique skills and experiences to the table.

In the film, Timothy Hutton brilliantly brings to life the characters of Thad Beaumont and George Stark, showcasing his remarkable acting range. Beaumont, a stereotypical writer, is portrayed as a clumsy and mild-mannered individual. Stark, on the other hand, is a confident and creepy physical entity. The stark contrast between these characters highlights Hutton's versatility.

Hutton's performance in "The Dark Half" is a reflection of his significant contributions to the film industry. He made history as the youngest recipient of the Academy Award for Best Supporting Actor for his role in "Ordinary People" (1980). His diverse roles in films like "Taps" (1981), "The Falcon and the Snowman" (1985), and "The Dark Half" (1993) further demonstrate his acting prowess.

Hutton's career took off with "Ordinary People", his first feature film. His portrayal of a guilt-ridden son in the film earned him both a Golden Globe Award and an Oscar. He continued to impress with his performances in "A Long Way Home" (1981) and "Taps" (1981), earning Golden Globe nominations for both.

Amy Madigan delivers a compelling performance as Liz Beaumont, the wife of Thad Beaumont. Despite her initial lack of understanding of Thad's struggle with his alter ego, Stark, she shows remarkable resolve when faced with adversity.

Madigan's contributions to cinema are both significant and diverse. She earned an Academy Award nomination for her role in "Twice in a Lifetime" (1985). Her filmography includes memorable roles in films like "Love Child" (1982), "Places in the Heart" (1984), "Field of Dreams" (1989), "Uncle Buck" (1989), "Pollock" (2000), and "Gone Baby Gone" (2007). Her television work is equally impressive, with a Golden Globe-winning performance in the television film "Roe vs. Wade" (1989).

Madigan's performance in "The Dark Half" and her broader contributions to the film world highlight her ability to bring complex characters to life. Her performances have earned her widespread recognition and solidified her place in film history.

Michael Rooker delivers a compelling performance as Sheriff Alan Pangborn. Despite evidence pointing towards Thad Beaumont as the perpetrator, Pangborn, a conscientious lawman, grapples with the unbelievable tale of an evil twin.

Rooker's contributions to cinema are both significant and diverse. He gained recognition for his role in "Henry: Portrait of a Serial Killer" (1986). His portrayal of Merle Dixon in "The Walking Dead" (2010–2013) and Yondu Udonta in "Guardians of the Galaxy" (2014) are among his most notable performances. His filmography also includes films like "Eight Men Out", "Mississippi Burning", "JFK", "Sea of Love", "Days of Thunder", "Cliffhanger", and "Tombstone".

Robert Joy delivers a compelling performance as Fred Clawson, a character who attempts to blackmail Thad Beaumont. This role adds an intriguing layer of tension to the film.

Joy's contributions to cinema are both significant and diverse. He is best known for his role in the series CSI: NY, and his performances in films like "Atlantic City" (1980), "Ragtime" (1981), "Desperately Seeking Susan" (1985), "Land of the Dead" (2005), and "The Hills Have Eyes" (2006). His work has earned him two Genie Award nominations for Best Supporting Actor. Additionally, Joy has made significant contributions to stage performances, particularly in Shakespearean productions.

Each of these actors brought their own unique flair to "The Dark Half", making it a memorable piece of cinema that continues to captivate audiences to this day.

The Cast and Performances

Timothy Hutton delivers a captivating performance in the dual role of Thad Beaumont and George Stark, showcasing his versatility as an actor. The supporting cast, including Amy Madigan, Michael Rooker, and Julie Harris, adds depth and intensity to the story. Romero's direction allows the cast to fully embody their characters and bring the psychological turmoil to life.

Reception and Legacy

"The Dark Half" received mixed reviews upon its release, with some praising Romero's faithful adaptation of King's novel and the performances of the cast, while others felt that the film lacked the same impact as the source material. Nevertheless, "The Dark Half" remains a notable entry in Romero's filmography, showcasing his ability to tackle complex psychological themes within the horror genre.

"The Dark Half" serves as a reminder of Romero's contributions to the horror genre and his skill in adapting literary works for the screen. His collaboration with Stephen King resulted in a film that explores the darkest corners of the human psyche and the consequences of unleashing hidden desires. Romero's legacy as a master of horror is further solidified through films like "The Dark Half."

The film continues to resonate with fans today, thanks to its timeless themes and masterful storytelling. Despite being released almost three decades ago, the film's relevance remains intact, captivating audiences with its exploration of identity, duality, and the blurred lines between reality and fiction.

One of the film's enduring strengths lies in its ability to blur the lines between reality and fiction. As Thad's characters come to life, we are reminded of the power of storytelling and the impact it can have on our lives. "The Dark Half" challenges our perception of reality, making us question the boundaries between the tangible and the imaginary. This theme resonates strongly in today's world, where the lines between truth and fabrication are often blurred, particularly in the age of social media and online personas.

Furthermore, it explores the consequences of repressed creativity and the lengths individuals will go to protect their art. Thad's struggle to distance himself from George Stark highlights the internal battle between artistic expression and societal expectations. As fans of the film, we are reminded of the importance of embracing our creative impulses and the dangers of denying our true passions. The film serves as a powerful reminder that suppressing one's creativity can have dire consequences, urging us to nurture our artistic endeavors and embrace our authentic selves.

Another aspect that keeps "The Dark Half" relevant is its commentary on the power of fandom and the blurred boundaries between creators and their audience. The film showcases the obsessive nature of fandom, with George Stark's followers idolizing him to dangerous extremes. In an era where fan culture and celebrity worship are more prevalent than ever, the film's exploration of the dark side of fandom resonates deeply. It serves as a cautionary tale, reminding us of the importance of maintaining a healthy relationship with our idols and recognizing the humanity beneath their public personas.

Moreover, the film's enduring relevance can be attributed to George Romero's masterful direction and his ability to create a sense of unease and tension. Romero's atmospheric visuals and suspenseful storytelling keep viewers on the edge of their seats, even after multiple viewings. His skillful use of practical effects and practical makeup enhances the film's eerie atmosphere, making it a standout in the horror genre. Romero's influence can still be felt in contemporary horror filmmaking, making "The Dark Half" a significant piece of cinematic history.

In conclusion, "The Dark Half" continues to be meaningful to fans today due to its exploration of identity, duality, and the blurred lines between reality and fiction. Its timeless themes, combined with George Romero's masterful direction, ensure its relevance in the horror genre. The film's exploration of the consequences of repressed creativity and the power of fandom strikes a chord with audiences, urging us to embrace our authentic selves and maintain a healthy relationship with the art and artists we admire. "The Dark Half " remains as evidence to the enduring power of storytelling and its ability to challenge our perceptions of the world around us.

Romero's adaptation of Stephen King's novel, "The Dark Half," was released on April 23, 1993, the film was brought to audiences by Orion Pictures in the United States and Columbia TriStar Film Distributors International on the global stage.

Despite its chilling narrative and stellar performances, it garnered just over $10.6 million domestically. In its opening week, it ranked sixth at the box office, raking in a total of $3,250,883 from 1,563 theaters.

As the years passed, "The Dark Half" found its way into homes, first through a VHS release in 1993, then on DVD on September 28, 1999, and finally in the high-definition Blu-Ray format on November 18, 2014.

While the film has been re-released in various formats over the years, the content has remained the same, preserving Romero's original vision. These re-releases serve to keep the film current with the latest home viewing technology, ensuring that it continues to reach and terrify new generations of horror fans.

Chapter 14: "Bruiser" Migration to Canada

A New Beginning in the Great White North

After making a significant impact on the horror genre with his zombie films, George A. Romero decided to explore new horizons and expand his creative endeavors. In the late 1990s, Romero made the decision to migrate to Canada, a country known for its thriving film industry and diverse cultural landscape. This move marked a new chapter in Romero's career and opened up a world of opportunities for the master of horror.

A Different Setting, a Fresh Perspective

Romero's decision to move to Canada was not only driven by the desire to explore new filmmaking possibilities but also by personal reasons. Canada offered a fresh canvas for Romero, allowing him to experiment with different storytelling techniques and explore themes that resonated with the Canadian audience. The change in location provided him with a unique perspective that would influence his future projects.

"Bruiser": Romero's Canadian Connection

One of the notable films that emerged from Romero's Canadian connection was "Bruiser" (2000). Filmed entirely in Toronto, "Bruiser" marked Romero's return to the realm of psychological horror. The film tells the story of Henry Creedlow, a man who wakes up one day to find his face completely blank, devoid of any identity. As Henry grapples with his newfound anonymity, he embarks on a journey of self-discovery and revenge.

"Bruiser" delves deep into themes of identity, alienation, and the masks we wear in society. It showcases Romero's ability to explore the human psyche and question societal norms. The film received mixed reviews from critics but remains a fascinating entry in Romero's filmography, showcasing his willingness to take risks and explore new territory.

During his time in Canada, Romero also had the opportunity to collaborate with talented Canadian actors and crew members. This collaboration enriched his work and brought fresh perspectives to his storytelling. Romero embraced the talent pool available in Canada and recognized the importance of diverse voices in his films.

Jason Flemyng delivers a compelling performance as Henry Creedlow, a character who is often overlooked and taken advantage of. This role allows Flemyng to showcase his ability to portray complex characters, as Creedlow embarks on a journey of self-discovery and revenge.

Flemyng's contributions to cinema are both significant and diverse. He is known for his collaborations with British filmmakers Guy Ritchie and Matthew Vaughn, appearing in films like "Lock, Stock and Two Smoking Barrels" (1998) and "Snatch" (2000). His performances in Hollywood productions such as "Rob Roy" (1995), "From Hell" (2001), "The League of Extraordinary Gentlemen" (2003), and "The Curious Case of Benjamin Button" (2008) further demonstrate his acting prowess.

Flemyng's performance in "Bruiser" and his broader contributions to the film world highlight his exceptional acting skills. His ability to bring diverse characters to life has earned him widespread recognition and solidified his place in film history.

Swedish actor Peter Stormare, renowned for his intense and often enigmatic performances, made a significant impact in the 2000 French-Canadian horror-thriller film "Bruiser". Directed by George A. Romero, Stormare played Milo Styles, a domineering boss at a local magazine company. His portrayal added a layer of complexity and intrigue to the film.

Stormare's career extends beyond "Bruiser". He has appeared in a wide array of films, showcasing his ability to adapt to various characters and contexts. His roles often span different nationalities, demonstrating his range as an actor and his commitment to his craft.

Starting his career at the Royal National Theatre of Sweden, Stormare spent eleven years honing his skills. He later became the Associate Artistic Director at the Tokyo Globe Theatre, directing many Shakespeare plays. This theatre background influenced his approach to film acting, allowing him to bring depth and nuance to his characters.

In addition to acting, Stormare has also made significant contributions as a playwright and a theater director. His work in theatre demonstrates his understanding of character development and storytelling, skills that he has successfully transferred to his film roles.

Whether he is playing a German in "The Big Lebowski", an Italian in "Prison Break", or a Russian in "Armageddon", Stormare brings authenticity to his roles. His performances, marked by their intensity and depth, have left an indelible mark on the film industry.

Leslie Hope, a Canadian actress and director, is best known for her role as Teri Bauer on the Fox television series "24". She has also made a name for herself as a successful entrepreneur, running an antique furniture store and design business.

Nina Garbiras, an American actress, is best known for her role as Andrea Little on the first season of NBC's award-winning series "Boomtown". Her acting career began in the chorus of a performance of "La traviata" at the Opera San José.

Andrew Tarbet made his mark on both stage and screen. His first movie role was in "The Detective", which starred Frank Sinatra.

Each of these actors brought their own unique flair to "Bruiser", making it a memorable addition to George A. Romero's filmography.

George Romero's "Bruiser" stands as an endorsement to the enduring power of the genre, exploring themes of identity, alienation, and the consequences of societal pressures. This chapter delves into the reasons why "Bruiser" remains meaningful and relevant to fans, transcending the boundaries of time.

At its core, "Bruiser" presents a haunting reflection on the masks we wear in our daily lives. The protagonist, Henry Creedlow, portrayed masterfully by Jason Flemyng, is a man trapped in a suffocating existence. As an unassuming everyman, he endures constant disrespect and humiliation from those around him. However, a surreal twist of fate occurs when he wakes up one morning to discover his face has been replaced by a blank white mask. This allegorical transformation serves as a metaphor for the anonymity that many individuals experience in society, where their true selves are hidden behind a facade.

Romero's skillful direction and thought-provoking screenplay delve deep into the psychological implications of Henry's transformation. As he navigates this new existence, devoid of his facial expressions and personal identity, he becomes a vessel for the audience's own fears and anxieties. We are forced to confront our own masked selves, questioning the authenticity of our actions and the masks we wear to conform to societal norms. In this way, "Bruiser" serves as a mirror, compelling us to examine our own lives and the masks we don to fit into a world that often demands conformity.

The film's exploration of alienation strikes a chord with audiences, as it taps into the universal longing for connection and understanding. Henry's journey from an unnoticed bystander to a vengeful anti-hero resonates with those who have felt marginalized or overlooked. Romero's portrayal of Henry's transformation into a fearless avenger provides a cathartic release for viewers who have experienced similar emotions of powerlessness and frustration. "Bruiser" offers a sense of empowerment, reminding us that even the most invisible among us possess the potential for strength and retribution.

Moreover, the film's social commentary remains relevant in today's society, where the pressure to conform and fit into predetermined molds is ever-present. Romero's biting critique of consumerism, corporate greed, and the dehumanizing effects of capitalism strikes a chord in an era defined by rampant materialism and the erosion of individuality. "Bruiser" challenges us to question the cost of assimilation and the toll it takes on our sense of self-worth.

In addition to its thematic depth, "Bruiser" boasts an atmospheric and visually striking aesthetic that further enhances its enduring appeal. Romero's directorial prowess shines through in every frame, creating a dark and foreboding world that mirrors Henry's internal turmoil. The use of shadow and light, combined with a haunting score, heightens the sense of unease and tension throughout the film. These artistic choices, combined with the compelling performances of the cast, elevate "Bruiser" beyond a mere horror movie, transforming it into a cinematic experience that lingers in the minds of viewers long after the credits roll.

"Bruiser" remains a significant and meaningful film for horror enthusiasts and cinephiles alike. Its exploration of identity, alienation, and societal pressures transcends the limitations of time, offering a timeless narrative that continues to resonate with audiences. Through its thought-provoking themes, powerful performances, and striking visuals, "Bruiser" stands as a testament to the enduring power of cinema to challenge, provoke, and captivate. It serves as a reminder that even in a world of masks, our true selves, and the battles we face, are what make us truly human.

But what truly sets "Bruiser" apart is its audacious exploration of the human condition. Romero fearlessly dives into the darkest recesses of the human soul, dissecting themes of identity, power, and the price of conformity. The enigmatic protagonist, Henry Creedlow, undergoes a metaphysical transformation that serves as a catalyst for the exploration of these profound concepts. Audiences are left pondering the masks they wear in their own lives and the hidden truths that lie beneath the surface.

The film's enduring relevance lies in its ability to tap into universal fears and anxieties. Henry's struggle against a world that seeks to suffocate his individuality strikes a chord with anyone who has ever felt oppressed or silenced. Romero's incisive social commentary exposes the façade of conformity, consumerism, and corporate greed, forcing us to confront the uncomfortable truths that lurk beneath the surface of society.

Furthermore, "Bruiser" boasts a cast that delivers performances of unparalleled brilliance. Jason Flemyng's portrayal of Henry Creedlow is a tour de force, capturing the character's internal turmoil and transformation with raw intensity. The supporting cast, including Peter Stormare and Leslie Hope, adds layers of complexity to the film, elevating it to heights rarely achieved in the horror genre.

To fully appreciate the genius of "Bruiser," one must also acknowledge its mesmerizing soundtrack. The haunting melodies and eerie soundscapes, composed by Donald Rubinstein, weave seamlessly into the film's fabric, heightening the tension and leaving an indelible mark on the viewer's subconscious.

In conclusion, "Bruiser" stands as evidence to George Romero's unparalleled genius and his ability to transcend the boundaries of conventional filmmaking. Its exploration of identity, power, and conformity resonates with audiences on a profound level, making it a timeless masterpiece that continues to captivate fans to this day. With its visionary direction, powerful performances, and thought-provoking themes, "Bruiser" remains an essential watch for anyone seeking a truly transformative cinematic experience.

George A. Romero's migration to Canada left a lasting impact on his career and the Canadian film industry. His decision to explore new storytelling avenues and collaborate with Canadian talent showcased his versatility as a filmmaker. Romero's presence in Canada also helped elevate the country's film industry and attract international attention.

Romero's time in Canada may have been relatively short, but it served as a significant chapter in his life and career. It allowed him to expand his artistic horizons, connect with a new audience, and leave a lasting mark on Canadian cinema.

The film made its way into American homes on October 9, 2001, through a DVD release.

Chapter 15: Land of the Dead: A World Divided by Class

In this chapter, we delve into George A. Romero's film "Land of the Dead," released in 2005. This post-apocalyptic horror film takes a critical look at the division of society based on class and power. Set in a world overrun by zombies, "Land of the Dead" presents a grim vision of a society divided between the privileged elite and the oppressed working class. This chapter will explore the themes, plot, and social commentary present in "Land of the Dead," highlighting Romero's critique of inequality and the consequences it brings.

"Land of the Dead" is set in a post-apocalyptic Pittsburgh-ish looking world, yet filmed in Canada, where zombies have taken over the majority of civilization. The remaining humans have sought refuge in a fortified city called Fiddler's Green, which is controlled by a wealthy ruling class. The city is a stark contrast to the decaying and dangerous world outside its walls, providing safety and luxury for the privileged few.

The film follows a group of scavengers led by Riley, a skilled soldier, and his loyal friend Cholo, as they venture into the zombie-infested wasteland to gather supplies. However, tensions rise as the working-class residents of the city, led by a charismatic figure named Kaufman, begin to question their place in society and the power dynamics at play.

A World Divided by Class

A central theme in "Land of the Dead" is the stark division of society based on class and power. The ruling elite residing in Fiddler's Green live lives of luxury and excess, while the working-class residents struggle to survive outside the city's confines. This stark contrast highlights the inequality and exploitation prevalent in the post-apocalyptic world.

Through the character of Kaufman, Romero presents a character who represents the ruling class. Kaufman maintains his power by controlling the resources and manipulating the fears of the working class. The film's exploration of class division serves as a critique of the real-world wealth gap and the ways in which those in power exploit and oppress the less fortunate.

Social Commentary and Critique

As with many of Romero's films, "Land of the Dead" is not just a zombie horror film but also a vehicle for social commentary. The film serves as a critique of capitalism, consumerism, and the inherent power imbalances that emerge in society. Romero uses the metaphor of the zombie apocalypse to shed light on the ways in which class divisions and inequality persist even in the face of a seemingly equalizing force.

Romero's critique extends beyond the divide between the rich and the poor. He also explores the dehumanizing effects of a society driven by greed and self-interest. The film challenges the audience to question the values and systems that perpetuate social inequality, urging us to consider the consequences of our actions and the potential for change.

Character Study: Riley and Cholo

The characters of Riley and Cholo provide a lens through which the audience experiences the world of "Land of the Dead" and its class divisions. Riley, a skilled soldier, represents the working-class struggle against the ruling elite. He is driven by a desire for justice and equality, determined to challenge the status quo. Cholo, on the other hand, initially seeks personal gain and power within the existing system but eventually realizes the oppression and corruption inherent in it.

Through these characters, Romero explores the complexities of navigating a world divided by class. Their journeys reflect the internal conflicts faced by individuals who find themselves caught between survival and fighting for a more just society.

Cinematic Techniques and Visuals

Romero's use of cinematic techniques in "Land of the Dead" adds depth and intensity to the film's social commentary. The gritty and desolate visuals of the post-apocalyptic landscape serve as a stark reminder of the world outside the city's walls. The juxtaposition between the opulence of Fiddler's Green and the decay of the outside world highlights the stark divide between the privileged and the oppressed.

Additionally, the portrayal of the zombies in "Land of the Dead" reflects the dehumanization and commodification of the working class. The zombies, often referred to as "the dead," represent the marginalized.

Australian actor Simon Baker, known for his versatility and depth, left a significant mark in the 2005 post-apocalyptic horror film "Land of the Dead". Baker played Riley Denbo, a resourceful leader who ventures into zombie-infested areas to scavenge for supplies. His portrayal added complexity and intrigue to the film.

Baker's career extends beyond "Land of the Dead". He has appeared in a wide array of films, showcasing his ability to adapt to various characters and contexts. His roles often span different genres, demonstrating his range as an actor and his commitment to his craft.

Starting his career in Australia, Baker acted in various television shows before relocating to the United States in the mid-90s. This television background influenced his approach to film acting, allowing him to bring depth and nuance to his characters.

In addition to acting, Baker has also made significant contributions as a director. He made his directorial debut with the 2017 film "Breath", which he also starred in, co-wrote and co-produced. His work in directing demonstrates his understanding of character development and storytelling, skills that he has successfully transferred to his film roles.

Whether he is playing a character in "The Ring Two", "Land of the Dead", or "The Devil Wears Prada", Baker brings authenticity to his roles. His performances, marked by their intensity and depth, have left an indelible mark on the film industry.

John Leguizamo, a dynamic actor known for his versatility, left a significant mark in the 2005 horror film "Land of the Dead". Leguizamo played Cholo DeMora, a hardened mercenary who ventures into zombie-infested areas. His portrayal added complexity and intrigue to the film.

Leguizamo's career extends beyond "Land of the Dead". He has appeared in over 100 films, produced over 20 films and documentaries, made over 30 television appearances, and has produced various television projects. His roles often span different genres, demonstrating his range as an actor and his commitment to his craft.

Starting his career as a stand-up comedian in New York City, Leguizamo rose to fame with major roles in films like "Super Mario Bros." and "Carlito's Way". This background influenced his approach to film acting, allowing him to bring depth and nuance to his characters.

Whether he is playing Luigi in "Super Mario Bros.", Benny Blanco in "Carlito's Way", or Cholo DeMora in "Land of the Dead", Leguizamo brings authenticity to his roles. His performances, marked by their intensity and depth, have left an indelible mark on the film industry.

Dennis Hopper played a crucial role in "Land of the Dead". Hopper portrayed Paul Kaufman, a ruthless ruler of a walled city. Hopper's career extends beyond "Land of the Dead". Known for his roles as mentally disturbed outsiders and rebels, he earned prizes from the Cannes Film Festival and Venice International Film Festival, as well as nominations for two Academy Awards, a Primetime Emmy Award, and two Golden Globe Awards.

Starting his career as a teenager in San Diego, California, Hopper quickly secured his first significant film role in "Rebel Without a Cause". Despite tales of his temperamental on-set antics, Hopper was then cast in a string of films, including "Giant" and "The Story of Mankind".

In addition to acting, Hopper has also made significant contributions as a director and writer. He directed and starred in "Easy Rider", winning an award at the Cannes Film Festival and was nominated for an Academy Award for Best Writing.

Whether he is playing Paul Kaufman in "Land of the Dead", a mentally disturbed outsider in "Easy Rider", or a rebel in another film, Hopper brings authenticity to his roles. His performances, marked by their intensity and depth, have left an indelible mark on the film industry.

Italian actress and filmmaker Asia Argento made a significant impact on the film. Argento portrayed Slack, a resourceful mercenary. Argento's career extends beyond "Land of the Dead". She has had roles in several films, produced various projects, and received numerous accolades. Her roles often span different genres, demonstrating her range as an actor and her commitment to her craft.

In addition to acting, Argento has also made significant contributions as a director and writer. She directed and starred in "The Heart Is Deceitful Above All Things", demonstrating her understanding of character development and storytelling.

Whether she is playing Slack in "Land of the Dead", a Russian undercover spy in "XXX", or a queen in "Marie Antoinette", Argento brings authenticity to her roles. Her performances, marked by their intensity and depth, have left an indelible mark on the film industry.

Canadian actor Robert Joy made a significant impact in the 2005 horror film "Land of the Dead". Directed by George A. Romero, Joy portrayed Charlie Houx, a resourceful mercenary. His portrayal added complexity to the film.

Joy's career extends beyond "Land of the Dead". Known for his roles as mentally disturbed outsiders and rebels, he earned prizes from the Cannes Film Festival and Venice International Film Festival, as well as nominations for two Academy Awards, a Primetime Emmy Award, and two Golden Globe Awards.

Starting his career in Montreal, Quebec, Canada, Joy quickly secured his first significant roles. Despite tales of his temperamental on-set antics, Joy was then cast in a string of films, showcasing his versatility.

Whether he is playing Charlie Houx in "Land of the Dead", a medical examiner in "CSI: NY", or a punk musician in "Desperately Seeking Susan", Joy brings authenticity to his roles. His performances, marked by their intensity and depth, have left an indelible mark on the film industry.

Eugene Clark, an American-Canadian actor, made a significant impact in the 2005 horror film "Land of the Dead". Directed by George A. Romero, Clark portrayed Big Daddy, an intelligent zombie leading an organized attack on the city. His portrayal added complexity to the film.

Clark's career extends beyond "Land of the Dead". He has had roles in numerous television productions and films, and received a Gemini Award for Best Supporting Actor in a Dramatic Series for his work on the hit TV series "Night Heat".

Starting his career in Tampa, Florida, Clark quickly secured his first significant roles. Despite tales of his temperamental on-set antics, Clark was then cast in a string of films, showcasing his versatility.

Whether he is playing Big Daddy in "Land of the Dead", Sid Gomez in "Tek War", or a character in "Night Heat", Clark brings authenticity to his roles. His performances, marked by their intensity and depth, have left an indelible mark on the film industry. I consider Big Daddy to be the last of the 'iconic', and memorable zombies, in George's films.

As the fourth installment in Romero's six-part "Living Dead" series, it follows the chilling narratives of "Night of the Living Dead", "Dawn of the Dead", and "Day of the Dead", and paves the way for "Diary of the Dead" and "Survival of the Dead".

With a budget of $15–19 million, the highest in Romero's Dead series, the film grossed an impressive $46 million. Set against the backdrop of a zombie-ridden Pittsburgh, Pennsylvania, the plot unfolds in a world where a feudal-like government holds sway.

The film's enduring legacy is anchored in its innovative portrayal of the evolution of zombies and their journey to Fiddler's Green. It introduced audiences to Big Daddy, an intelligent zombie leader, leaving his fate tantalizingly unresolved at the film's conclusion.

"Land of the Dead" is peppered with sublime in-jokes, including the reprisal of Tom Savini's biker zombie from 'Dawn of the Dead'. The legacy of the film is set to continue with "Twilight of the Dead", a concluding chapter intended to be Romero's final statement on the genre. This film, much like its predecessors, promises to keep audiences on the edge of their seats, eagerly anticipating the next twist in the tale.

Released in 2005, George Romero's "Land of the Dead" has cemented itself as a beloved film among fans of the zombie genre. Its enduring popularity can be attributed to several factors that continue to resonate with audiences today. In this chapter, we will explore why fans enjoy "Land of the Dead" and why it remains relevant in the hearts of horror enthusiasts.

"Land of the Dead" offers a captivating narrative that goes beyond the typical zombie tropes. Romero's storytelling prowess shines through as he weaves a tale of survival, societal decay, and moral complexity. Fans appreciate the film's ability to present thought-provoking themes within the horror genre, elevating it beyond mere mindless violence. Its engaging plot keeps viewers invested from start to finish, making it a compelling viewing experience.

Romero's films have always been known for their social commentary, and "Land of the Dead" is no exception. The film explores themes of class struggle and wealth disparity, drawing parallels to real-world issues. Fans appreciate its ability to shed light on societal flaws and challenge the status quo, making it a relevant commentary on the world we live in. The film's social critique continues to resonate with fans who seek horror with substance.

"Land of the Dead" introduces a diverse cast of characters, each with their own unique traits and motivations. From the morally driven Riley to the complex anti-hero Cholo, fans are drawn to these well-developed characters who navigate a world consumed by chaos. Their struggles and personal journeys add depth to the story and provide emotional investment for viewers. Fans find themselves rooting for their favorite characters and connecting with their triumphs and tragedies.

The film offers a plethora of unforgettable moments that have left a lasting impact on fans. From the thrilling action sequences to the striking practical effects, "Land of the Dead" delivers visceral and intense scenes that keep viewers on the edge of their seats. Whether it's the harrowing encounters with hordes of zombies or the explosive clashes between survivors, these moments of high tension and adrenaline provide an exhilarating experience for fans of the genre.

"Land of the Dead" holds a special place in the hearts of fans due to its significant contributions to the zombie genre. It continues the legacy of Romero's "Dead" series, building upon the foundation laid by its predecessors. The film's impact can be seen in subsequent zombie films and TV shows, as it set a benchmark for storytelling and social commentary within the genre. Its influence continues to inspire filmmakers and keeps the film relevant in the eyes of fans.

The enduring appeal of "Land of the Dead" lies in its elevated storytelling, thought-provoking social commentary, memorable characters, and unforgettable moments of horror. Fans continue to enjoy the film because of its ability to captivate and engage, providing a unique viewing experience within the zombie genre. As long as viewers seek a blend of thrills, substance, and societal critique, "Land of the Dead" will remain relevant and cherished by fans for years to come.

In the eerie aftermath of a world ravaged by the undead, the fourth installment of George A. Romero's six-part Living Dead series, "Land of the Dead", emerged from the shadows. This post-apocalyptic horror masterpiece was unveiled to North American audiences on June 24, 2005, under the banner of Universal Pictures.

Despite its chilling premise, the film ignited the box office, devouring a gross of $46.8 million against a budget of $15–19 million. The domestic appetite accounted for $20,700,082, while international audiences contributed a further $26,374,051.

As the echoes of the cinema experience faded, "Land of the Dead" clawed its way into homes. The DVD version made its chilling debut in U.S. homes on October 18, 2005. The Blu-Ray version, offering crystal clear terror, was released much later on October 31, 2017, and in the UK on February 15, 2021.

Chapter 16: Diary of the Dead: Found Footage in the Zombie Genre

In this chapter, we will dive deep into "Diary of the Dead," George A. Romero's found footage film that stands out as a unique addition to the zombie genre. We will explore the origins of found footage in cinema, the narrative structure of "Diary of the Dead," and the impact of this filmmaking technique on the overall viewing experience.

Origins of Found Footage in Cinema

The concept of found footage in cinema can be traced back to the 1980 film "Cannibal Holocaust" directed by Ruggero Deodato. This controversial film employed a pseudo-documentary style, presenting itself as recovered footage from a group of missing filmmakers. The film's realistic approach caused a stir and became a precursor to the found footage genre.

However, it was not until the late 1990s and early 2000s that found footage gained mainstream popularity with films like "The Blair Witch Project" (1999) and "Paranormal Activity" (2007). These films used a combination of handheld cameras and first-person perspectives to create a sense of realism and immediacy, making viewers feel like they were part of the story.

"Diary of the Dead": A New Perspective on the Zombie Genre

"Diary of the Dead" takes the found footage concept and applies it to the zombie genre, offering a fresh take on Romero's signature storytelling. The film follows a group of university students who document the outbreak of the zombie apocalypse as it unfolds. The use of found footage in "Diary of the Dead" allows the audience to experience the chaos and fear of the situation firsthand.

The narrative structure of the film revolves around the character of Jason, a film student who decides to document the events as they happen. He records everything that unfolds, from the initial reports of the dead returning to life to the group's struggle for survival. This approach provides a voyeuristic perspective, blurring the line between the viewers and the characters on screen.

Immersion and Realism in "Diary of the Dead"

The found footage technique in "Diary of the Dead" enhances the sense of immersion and realism. The shaky camera movements, imperfect framing, and raw audio capture the urgency and intensity of the characters' experiences. The use of amateur cinematography adds an authentic touch, as the characters are not professional filmmakers but ordinary individuals caught in extraordinary circumstances.

The film also incorporates various sources of footage, including news broadcasts, security cameras, and personal recordings, which further contribute to the realism. These different perspectives provide a fragmented and multi-faceted view of the unfolding events, giving the audience a comprehensive understanding of the situation.

Social Commentary and Critique

As with many of Romero's films, "Diary of the Dead" contains social commentary and critique. The found footage style allows Romero to explore contemporary issues such as media manipulation, misinformation, and the voyeuristic nature of society. By presenting the events through the lens of the characters' cameras, Romero highlights the power dynamics between those who control the narrative and those who are merely passive observers.

The film also raises questions about the role of media in shaping public perception during times of crisis. As the characters encounter various news reports and witness the distortion of information, Romero challenges the audience to question the reliability of what they see and hear. This commentary remains relevant in today's age of social media and the spread of fake news.

"Diary of the Dead" is a 2007 film by George A. Romero that brought together a diverse and talented cast. Let's delve into the lives of these remarkable actors:

Canadian actress Michelle Morgan, renowned for her role as Lou Fleming on the CBC series Heartland, made her significant debut in the film. Her portrayal of the lead character, Debra Moynihan, was a game-changer in her career, offering her a stage to display her versatility and talent.

In the film, Debra, the group's filmmaker, is determined to document everything. Morgan's performance of Debra was remarkable for its depth, successfully blending vulnerability and strength. This performance added a layer of complexity to the horror genre, enhancing the film's overall impact.

Morgan's connection with Debra is evident in her performance. She brings a sense of realism and relatability to the role, making Debra a memorable character in the film. This connection between actor and character is a testament to Morgan's skill and dedication as an actress.

Morgan's contributions to the film world extend beyond Diary of the Dead. She has expanded her career to include directing and writing. Her first short film, "Mi Madre, My Father" (2017), was selected by Telefilm for the "Not Short on Talent at Cannes" for the Cannes Film Festival short film corner. This achievement highlights her versatility and talent in various aspects of filmmaking.

Canadian actor Joshua Close made his mark in the film industry with his role in the film. His character, Jason Creed, an enthusiastic film student documenting the zombie apocalypse, was a standout performance that showcased his talent and versatility.

Close's connection to Jason is evident in his performance, bringing a sense of realism to the role and making Jason a memorable character in the film. In the film, Jason grapples with his survival instincts and his responsibility towards the group. Close's portrayal of this struggle adds depth to his character and enhances the overall impact of the film.

Close's contributions to the film world extend beyond Diary of the Dead. He has starred in numerous TV series and films, and his performance in "Thorne: Sleepyhead" won him a Gemini. He has worked with top directors like P.T. Anderson and Steven Spielberg and made his debut as Viktor Bokov in Kathryn Bigelow's film "K:19: The Widowmaker" alongside Harrison Ford.

Close has also made his mark on stage, most recently in Geffen's hit production of "The Lonely Few". He has written and directed films, and his work has been showcased internationally. These achievements highlight his versatility and talent in various aspects of filmmaking.

Shawn Roberts, renowned for his roles in zombie films such as Land of the Dead, Diary of the Dead, and the Resident Evil franchise, delivered a standout performance as Tony Ravello in Diary of the Dead. His portrayal of Tony, filled with realism and depth, made the character unforgettable and showcased Roberts' dedication and skill as an actor.

Beyond Diary of the Dead, Roberts has made significant contributions to the film world. His diverse roles, including the villainous Albert Wesker in the Resident Evil franchise and co-starring with Anna Paquin, highlight his versatility. His career, which began with a school play, has since flourished, balancing between television and film work.

His recent roles include Sam Langstone in Heartland, Adam Cauldfield in the Hallmark movie Love Under the Olive Tree, and Spartacus in the Season 6 premiere of Legends of Tomorrow. These roles further underscore his talent and versatility.

Amy Lalonde, made a significant impact in the film industry with her role as Tracy Thurman in the film. Her portrayal of Tracy, a Texas firecracker and a scream queen, was a standout performance that showcased her talent and versatility.

Lalonde's connection to Tracy is evident in her performance, bringing a sense of realism and relatability to the role and making Tracy a memorable character in the film. This connection is a testament to Lalonde's skill and dedication as an actress.

Beyond Diary of the Dead, Lalonde has made significant contributions to the film world. She has starred in numerous commercials and made guest appearances in various TV series. Her first two feature films were Heartstopper and 5ive Girls in 2006. She has also made TV Movie of the Week appearances, including Murder in the Hamptons, Earthstorm, Nature of the Beast (ABC Family), and CBC's Victor: The Victor Davis Story.

Joe Dinicol's character, Eliot, a tech dweeb, was a standout performance that showcased his talent and versatility. Dinicol's connection to Eliot is evident in his performance, bringing a sense of realism and relatability to the role and making Eliot a memorable character in the film. This connection is a testament to Dinicol's skill and dedication as an actor.

Beyond Diary of the Dead, Dinicol has made significant contributions to the film world. He has starred in numerous TV series and films, including Scott Pilgrim vs. the World and Passchendaele. His career, which began with a school play, has since flourished, balancing between television and film work.

His recent roles include Sam Langstone in Heartland, Adam Cauldfield in the Hallmark movie Love Under the Olive Tree, and Spartacus in the Season 6 premiere of Legends of Tomorrow. These roles further underscore his talent and versatility.

American actor Scott Wentworth, who later immigrated to Canada, portrayal of the character Andrew Maxwell, an alcoholic film professor, was a standout performance that showcased his talent and versatility.

Wentworth's connection to Maxwell is evident in his performance, bringing a sense of realism and relatability to the role and making Maxwell a memorable character in the film. This connection is a testament to Wentworth's skill and dedication as an actor.

Beyond Diary of the Dead, Wentworth has made significant contributions to the film world. He has starred in numerous TV series and films, including Scott Pilgrim vs. the World and Passchendaele. His career, which began with a school play, has since flourished, balancing between television and film work.

His recent roles include Sam Langstone in Heartland, Adam Cauldfield in the Hallmark movie Love Under the Olive Tree, and Spartacus in the Season 6 premiere of Legends of Tomorrow. These roles further underscore his talent and versatility.

Philip Riccio, a distinguished actor and director hailing from Toronto, Canada. His character, Ridley, a tech dweeb, was a standout performance that showcased his talent and versatility.

Riccio's connection to Ridley is evident in his performance, bringing a sense of realism and relatability to the role and making Ridley a memorable character in the film.

Beyond Diary of the Dead, Riccio has starred in numerous TV series and films, including Scott Pilgrim vs. the World and Passchendaele. His career, which began with a school play, has since flourished, balancing between television and film work

Each of these actors brought their unique talents and experiences to the film, contributing to the success of "Diary of the Dead".

Impact on the Zombie Genre

"Diary of the Dead" broke new ground in the zombie genre by introducing the found footage style. It influenced subsequent films and television shows within the genre, such as "REC" (2007), "Cloverfield" (2008), and "The Walking Dead" (2010-present). The use of found footage allows filmmakers to explore different perspectives and create a sense of immediacy, enabling viewers to feel more connected to the characters and their struggles.

By blending the found footage technique with the zombie genre, Romero breathed new life into his storytelling. "Diary of the Dead" stands as proof to his ability to innovate and push the boundaries of the genre he helped popularize.

A Timeless Reflection on Society and Survival. In the realm of horror films, there are few directors as influential and revered as George Romero. Known for his groundbreaking work in the zombie genre, Romero's 2007 film, Diary of the Dead, stands as a proclamation to his creative vision and storytelling prowess. Despite the passage of time, this film continues to captivate fans and remain relevant in today's cinematic landscape. It is a reflection of our society, a commentary on human nature, and a chilling exploration of survival in the face of chaos.

Diary of the Dead follows a group of film students who find themselves at the epicenter of a zombie outbreak. Armed with their cameras, they document the unfolding apocalypse, providing a unique perspective that sets the film apart from its predecessors. What makes this film resonate with fans is its ability to seamlessly blend horror with social commentary, forcing us to confront our own humanity in the face of an unimaginable threat.

One of the key reasons why Diary of the Dead remains meaningful to fans today is its examination of the media's role in shaping our perception of reality. In an era dominated by social media and citizen journalism, the film's portrayal of the students using their cameras to capture the truth resonates deeply. It raises important questions about the authenticity of information disseminated through various channels and how the truth can be distorted or manipulated to fit a particular narrative. This theme continues to hold relevance in our current age, where the proliferation of fake news and misinformation has become a pressing concern.

Diary delves into the human psyche and the lengths individuals will go to survive in a world gone mad. As the characters confront unimaginable horrors, they are forced to make difficult choices, testing their morality and revealing their true nature. This exploration of human behavior in extreme circumstances serves as a mirror, causing us to question our own capacity for compassion, desperation, and self-preservation. It serves as a stark reminder that, when pushed to the edge, even the most well-intentioned individuals can succumb to darkness.

Romero's film also stands out due to its gritty and realistic portrayal of the zombie apocalypse. Unlike many other zombie movies that focus solely on the gore and violence, Diary of the Dead infuses a sense of authenticity into its narrative. The handheld camera perspective provides an immersive experience, intensifying the sense of chaos and immediacy. This raw and unfiltered approach allows viewers to connect with the characters on a visceral level, drawing them deeper into the story and heightening the impact of its themes.

Diary challenges traditional gender roles and showcases strong and capable female characters. In a genre often criticized for its portrayal of women as helpless victims, Romero breaks the mold by presenting women who are resourceful, intelligent, and resilient. This refreshing depiction of female characters resonates with audiences and serves as a powerful reminder of the strength and agency possessed by women in the face of adversity.

Diary of the Dead continues to hold a special place in the hearts of horror fans for its thought-provoking exploration of society, its unflinching examination of human nature, and its immersive and authentic storytelling. By addressing relevant societal issues, challenging gender norms, and delving into the depths of the human psyche, this film remains timeless and meaningful, leaving an indelible mark on the genre. It serves as a chilling reminder that, even in the face of the undead, our greatest threats may lie within ourselves.

Diary holds an unparalleled position in the hearts of horror enthusiasts. This cinematic gem, even after years of its release, continues to mesmerize fans with its unique blend of terror and social commentary. The film's enduring relevance lies in its ability to delve deep into the human psyche, exploring the darkest corners of our existence, and presenting a chilling vision of survival in a world overrun by the undead.

Unlike other zombie flicks, Diary of the Dead takes a fresh approach by presenting the story through the lens of a group of film students armed with their cameras. This innovative perspective allows viewers to immerse themselves in the chaos and brutality unfolding on screen, making the horror all the more palpable. The film's found-footage style creates an atmosphere of authenticity, making us feel like active participants in the terrifying events unfolding before our eyes.

What sets Diary of the Dead apart from its contemporaries is its unflinching examination of the media's influence on our perception of reality. Through the lens of the student filmmakers, the film reveals the power and pitfalls of modern media. In a world inundated with fake news and manipulated narratives, Diary serves as a cautionary tale, urging us to question the information we consume and the authenticity of the stories we believe. Its message resonates strongly in today's age of misinformation, reminding us of the importance of critical thinking and discernment.

The film offers a captivating exploration of the human condition and the lengths people are willing to go to survive. As the characters face the unimaginable horrors of the zombie apocalypse, they are forced to confront their own morality, making life-or-death decisions that shape their fates. This examination of human behavior under extreme circumstances is both harrowing and thought-provoking, forcing us to question our own capacity for heroism, sacrifice, and even brutality. Diary of the Dead is a mirror that reflects our deepest fears and desires, leaving an indelible mark on our psyche.

Romero's film also deserves praise for its strong and empowering portrayal of female characters. Breaking away from the traditional damsel-in-distress trope, Diary of the Dead presents women who are resourceful, intelligent, and capable of holding their own in the face of the undead. In a genre often criticized for its lack of meaningful female representation, this film stands as a testament to Romero's progressive vision and commitment to challenging societal norms.

Diary remains a timeless masterpiece that continues to captivate fans with its unique perspective, social commentary, and chilling portrayal of survival. Its exploration of the media's influence, its unflinching examination of the human condition, and its empowering portrayal of female characters make it a standout in the realm of horror cinema. As we revisit this film, we are reminded of the enduring power of storytelling and the impact it can have on our understanding of ourselves and the world around us.

February 15, 2008 distributed far and wide by The Weinstein Company. Despite its modest budget of $2 million, the film clawed its way to a respectable $5.3 million at the box office, proving once again that Romero's touch was golden.

As the film's theatrical run began to fade, "Diary" found a new life in the realm of home media. On May 20, 2008, Dimension Extreme and Genius Products released the film on DVD, allowing horror enthusiasts to bring the terror home. Not long after, on October 21, 2008, the film made its debut on Blu-Ray, offering viewers a high-definition glimpse into Romero's horrifying world.

Chapter 17: Survival of the Dead: Exploring the Moral Dilemma

In this chapter, we will delve into George A. Romero's film "Survival of the Dead" and examine the moral dilemma that lies at the heart of the story. We will explore the themes of human nature, societal divisions, and the struggle for survival in a world overrun by the undead.

"Survival of the Dead" takes place on an isolated island off the coast of Delaware, where two rival families, the O'Flynns and the Muldoons, find themselves in conflict over how to deal with the zombie outbreak.

The O'Flynns believe in exterminating the undead, while the Muldoons believe in finding a cure to restore their loved ones back to normal. This clash of ideologies sets the stage for the moral dilemma that the characters face.

Human Nature in Extreme Situations

Romero's films often explore the depths of human nature and how it is tested in the face of dire circumstances. "Survival of the Dead" is no exception. As the survivors on the island struggle to stay alive, tensions rise, and the line between right and wrong becomes blurred.

The film poses thought-provoking questions: How far are individuals willing to go to protect themselves and their loved ones? Can humanity remain intact in a world consumed by death and decay? Romero challenges the audience to reflect on the moral choices made by the characters and consider what they would do in their shoes.

Society's Divide and the Zombie Apocalypse

"Survival of the Dead" also explores the concept of societal divisions and how they persist even in the face of a common threat. The O'Flynns and the Muldoons represent two opposing factions, each with their own beliefs and strategies for survival. This division reflects real-world conflicts and reminds us that even in the worst of times, humanity's differences can lead to further disarray.

Romero's depiction of these divisions forces the audience to confront the question of unity in the face of adversity. Can society come together to overcome the zombie apocalypse, or are we destined to succumb to our own internal conflicts?

Ethics and the Undead

One of the central ethical dilemmas in "Survival of the Dead" revolves around the treatment of the undead. The Muldoons believe that there is a possibility of finding a cure and restoring their loved ones back to normal, whereas the O'Flynns see the undead as a threat that must be eliminated. This conflict raises profound questions about the value of life, the nature of identity, and the limits of compassion.

Romero challenges our preconceptions by portraying the undead as beings who retain some semblance of their former selves. This creates a moral quandary for the characters and the audience alike. Is it ethical to kill these beings, even if they were once loved ones? What responsibility do we have to preserve life, even in the face of seemingly insurmountable odds?

In the world of cinema, the cast of a film can make or break its success. The 2009 film "Survival of the Dead" by George A. Romero was no exception. The film boasted a diverse and talented cast, each bringing their unique flair to the screen.

Alan van Sprang, delivered a memorable performance in the 2009 film as Sergeant "Nicotine" Crockett. This marked his second appearance in Romero's iconic zombie films.

In the film, Crockett is a former Colonel and the leader of a group of soldiers navigating a world overrun by zombies. Sprang's portrayal of this hardened character, shaped by the harsh realities of a post-apocalyptic world, stands in stark contrast to his previous roles, adding a layer of depth and complexity to his filmography.

Alan's performance in "Survival of the Dead" is marked by a sense of humanity and pragmatism, making his character relatable despite the horror film setting. His portrayal contributes to the film's exploration of moral ambiguity in a world where societal norms have been upended.

His contributions to the film world extend beyond this film. His diverse roles, ranging from Sir Francis Bryan in "The Tudors" to King Henry in "Reign" and Valentine Morgenstern in "Shadowhunters," showcase his versatility and talent. His collaborations with Romero, in particular, have solidified his standing in the horror film genre and contributed to the evolution of the zombie narrative.

Kenneth Welsh, a celebrated Canadian actor, brought to life the character of Patrick O'Flynn in the 2009 film "Survival of the Dead." His portrayal of O'Flynn, a man determined to eradicate the undead, added a layer of tension and complexity to the film's narrative. Despite the horror of the zombie apocalypse, Welsh's performance was imbued with a sense of humanity and determination, making O'Flynn a compelling character in a chaotic world.

Welsh's contributions to the film world extend far beyond this role. He has demonstrated his acting prowess in a variety of roles across film and television, from the villainous Windom Earle in "Twin Peaks" to acclaimed performances in "The Day After Tomorrow," "Adoration," and Martin Scorsese's "The Aviator." His ability to embody diverse characters and historical figures showcases his versatility and talent.

His work has not gone unnoticed. Welsh has been nominated for several awards, including two Genie Awards for Best Actor, and won the award for Best Supporting Actor at the 16th Genie Awards for "Margaret's Museum."

Canadian actress Kathleen Munroe, known for her diverse roles, made a significant contribution to the film through her portrayal of Janet O'Flynn. Set on Plum Island amidst a zombie apocalypse, the film explores the feud between two Irish families, the O'Flynns and the Muldoons. Munroe's character, caught in this conflict, adds a layer of complexity to the narrative.

Despite the horror of the situation, Munroe's performance is marked by a sense of humanity and determination, making O'Flynn a compelling character. This depth of character is a testament to Munroe's acting prowess and her ability to bring her characters to life.

Beyond this film, Munroe's contributions to the film world are significant. She has demonstrated her versatility and talent in a variety of roles across film and television. Her performances have been widely acclaimed, showcasing her ability to embody diverse characters. Munroe's talent has not gone unnoticed. She won the 2010 ACTRA Award for Outstanding Female Performance, further cementing her place in the industry.

From the chilling realms of the undead to the humorous escapades of a wimpy kid, Devon Bostick's cinematic journey is nothing short of extraordinary. Born in the heart of Canada, Bostick's acting prowess was evident from his early roles, one of which was the enigmatic "Boy" in the 2009 film "Survival of the Dead."

Bostick's character, a National Guard deserter, navigates a zombie-infested landscape. His portrayal of "Boy" is a masterclass in subtlety and depth, adding a unique layer to the narrative and exploring the essence of survival and humanity.

Bostick's versatility doesn't stop there. He brought laughter to millions as the mischievous Rodrick Heffley in the "Diary of a Wimpy Kid" series, showcasing his comedic flair. His role as Simon in "Adoration" displayed his ability to handle complex emotions, further solidifying his acting credentials.

His venture into dystopian science fiction with "The 100" series, where he played Jasper Jordan, one of the original 100 young prisoners sent to Earth, demonstrated his ability to adapt to diverse roles and narratives.

Bostick's talent transcends mediums. He reprised his role as Rodrick Heffley in the animated series of "Diary of a Wimpy Kid," proving his adaptability and range.

Bostick's journey, from his humble beginnings in Toronto to his current success, serves as a beacon for aspiring actors. His dedication to his craft, his ability to breathe life into a wide array of characters, and his contributions to various genres underscore his significance in the film world.

Richard Fitzpatrick, a seasoned actor known for his diverse roles, has left an indelible mark on the film industry. His role as Seamus Muldoon in the 2009 film "Survival of the Dead" is particularly noteworthy.

In the film, Fitzpatrick's character, Muldoon, is caught in a family feud on Plum Island, off the coast of Delaware. The feud revolves around their contrasting views on handling the undead. Muldoon, believing in the possibility of a cure, advocates for preserving the undead, a stance that starkly contrasts with his adversary, Patrick O'Flynn, who believes in eliminating them.

Fitzpatrick's portrayal of Muldoon showcases his ability to bring depth to complex characters. He effectively captures Muldoon's sternness and unwavering belief in a potential cure, painting a vivid picture of a man grappling with moral dilemmas in a zombie apocalypse.

Fitzpatrick's contributions to the film world extend beyond his acting roles. He has filmed over 50 films for clients like the BBC, National Geographic, and Discovery Channel, demonstrating his prowess behind the camera.

Athena Karkanis, a distinguished actress of Greek and Egyptian heritage. In "Survival of the Dead", Karkanis' character is part of a team led by former Colonel and now Sergeant "Nicotine" Crockett. Her portrayal of Tomboy, a character who embodies both strength and vulnerability, adds a touch of authenticity to the film's post-apocalyptic setting.

Karkanis' career extends beyond this film, with notable roles in other horror films such as "Saw IV" (2007), "Repo! The Genetic Opera" (2008), "Saw VI" (2009), and "The Barrens" (2012). These roles have allowed her to delve into a variety of narratives and characters, solidifying her standing in the film industry.

In addition to horror films, Karkanis has showcased her versatility in action films like "The Art of War II: Betrayal" (2008), and "Sacrifice" (2011), as well as in numerous roles on Canadian television.

Karkanis' contributions to the film world are not limited to on-screen performances. Her voice acting work, including roles in "Skyland", "MetaJets", "Julius Jr.", "Total Drama: Revenge of the Island", "Dino Ranch" and "My Little Pony: Make Your Mark", demonstrates her wide-ranging talents. She was the lead voice for "Growing Up Creepie" and has a regular role in "Wild Kratts" as Aviva Corcovado.

In "Survival", Stefano Di Matteo's character is part of a team navigating a post-apocalyptic world on Plum Island. His portrayal of the National Guardsman is marked by depth and complexity, adding a touch of realism to the film's setting.

Di Matteo's filmography extends beyond this film, with notable roles in his hometown of Toronto and Vancouver. During his time in Vancouver, he appeared in a supporting role on "Cold Squad" as Manuel Diaz and quickly found himself in the pilot for the hit TV series "Stargate Atlantis", as Toran.

Upon returning to Toronto, Di Matteo continued to make his mark in the film industry. He has appeared in supporting roles on TV shows such as "Kevin Hill", "Beautiful People", and again as a miracle worker in the made-for-TV movie "Absolution", opposite Samantha Mathis.

Di Matteo's contributions to the film world extend beyond his on-screen performances. His directorial debut, "Communication Breakdown", a romantic comedy about the trials and tribulations of dating in the 21st century, had its world premiere at the Canadian Film Festival, followed by a screening at the prestigious Maui Film Festival, and eventually won him a Best Short Film award at the MIFF Festival.

Each of these actors brought their unique talents and experiences to "Survival of the Dead", contributing to the film's success and leaving a lasting impression on audiences worldwide.

The Impact of "Survival of the Dead"

"Survival" may not have received the same level of acclaim as some of Romero's earlier works, but it continues his tradition of using the zombie genre as a canvas for social commentary. By exploring the moral dilemmas faced by the characters, Romero invites us to reflect on our own values, principles, and the choices we would make in similar circumstances.

The film challenges our assumptions about right and wrong, humanity and monstrosity, and the lengths we would go to survive. It serves as a reminder that in the most extraordinary of circumstances, our moral compass can be tested, and our true nature revealed.

"Survival of the Dead" is known for his groundbreaking contributions to the zombie genre. While the movie may not have received the same level of acclaim as Romero's earlier works like "Night of the Living Dead" or "Dawn of the Dead," it still holds immense significance for fans today. Despite its mixed reception, "Survival of the Dead" remains relevant due to its unique take on the zombie apocalypse, thought-provoking themes, and Romero's continued influence on the genre.

At its core, "Survival" is a story about survival and the lengths people go to protect what they believe in. Set in a world overrun by zombies, the film follows a group of desperate survivors who stumble upon an island where two feuding families are engaged in an intense conflict. What sets this film apart from others in the genre is its exploration of the human condition amidst chaos. Romero uses the zombie outbreak as a backdrop to delve into deeper themes of tribalism, morality, and the destructive nature of human conflict.

One of the reasons "Survival of the Dead" remains meaningful to fans today is its exploration of tribalism and the idea that humans can be their own worst enemies. The film showcases how individuals can become so consumed by their beliefs and prejudices that they lose sight of the bigger picture. Romero's portrayal of the warring families on the island serves as a cautionary tale, reminding us of the dangers of division and the importance of unity in the face of adversity.

Furthermore, "Survival of the Dead" challenges our preconceived notions of right and wrong. It raises questions about the moral ambiguity of survival in a post-apocalyptic world. The film blurs the line between heroes and villains, forcing viewers to confront their own moral compasses. Romero's intention was never to provide easy answers but to spark conversations and introspection amongst the audience.

Romero's influence on the zombie genre cannot be overstated. His films pioneered the concept of the undead as a reflection of societal issues, and "Survival" is no exception. By presenting zombies not just as mindless creatures to be feared, but as beings capable of learning and adapting, Romero pushes the boundaries of the genre. He challenges us to consider the humanity that remains in the undead and question our own notions of what it means to be alive.

In addition to its thought-provoking themes, "Survival of the Dead" also showcases Romero's mastery of practical effects and his ability to create tension and suspense. The film is filled with intense action sequences, gruesome kills, and well-executed practical effects that immerse viewers in the terrifying world of the undead. Romero's commitment to practical effects over CGI adds a sense of authenticity and grittiness to the film, enhancing the overall viewing experience.

Despite its divisive reception, "Survival" is an assertion to George Romero's legacy and his impact on the zombie genre. Its unique take on the apocalypse, exploration of relevant themes, and Romero's directorial prowess make it a film that continues to resonate with fans today. While it may not have achieved the same level of recognition as some of his earlier works, "Survival of the Dead" stands as a reminder of Romero's unparalleled contribution to the world of horror cinema.

"Survival" is an absolute masterpiece that continues to captivate and enthrall fans to this day. The film's brilliance lies in its ability to seamlessly blend elements of horror, drama, and social commentary into a seamless narrative. George Romero's visionary direction elevates the film to new heights, making it a must-watch for any true cinephile.

The film's enduring relevance stems from its thought-provoking exploration of human nature in the face of a zombie apocalypse. Romero masterfully crafts a narrative that forces viewers to question their own morality and the lengths they would go to survive. The moral ambiguity of the characters challenges traditional notions of heroism and villainy, making for a gripping and intellectually stimulating viewing experience.

What truly sets "Survival" apart is its innovative take on the undead themselves. Romero breaks free from the shackles of conventional zombie tropes and introduces a fresh perspective. The zombies in this film are not mere mindless creatures but sentient beings capable of learning and adapting. This reinvention of the genre adds a new layer of complexity and intrigue, making it a standout film in the zombie canon.

Romero's unparalleled mastery of practical effects is on full display in "Survival of the Dead." The visceral and realistic portrayal of violence and gore adds an undeniable authenticity to the film. Every gruesome kill and intense action sequence is brought to life with meticulous attention to detail. This commitment to practical effects sets the film apart from its CGI-laden counterparts and ensures a truly immersive and terrifying experience for the audience.

The film's exploration of tribalism and the destructive nature of human conflict remains incredibly relevant in today's society. Romero uses the backdrop of a zombie outbreak to shed light on the dangers of division and the importance of unity. The feuding families on the island serve as a powerful metaphor for the destructive consequences of blind loyalty and prejudice. This underlying social commentary adds depth and substance to the film, elevating it beyond mere entertainment.

"Survival of the Dead" is a film that continues to captivate and resonate with fans due to its unique take on the zombie genre, thought-provoking themes, and Romero's directorial brilliance. Its enduring relevance lies in its ability to challenge societal norms, provoke introspection, and provide an immersive and thrilling viewing experience.

The film released on September 9th, 2009, distributed by Magnet Releasing and Entertainment One Films, was a test of Romero's ability to captivate audiences with his unique blend of horror and social commentary. Despite its modest budget of $4 million, the film managed to gross $386,078 at the box office.

UK audiences were the first to take home a piece of the horror, with the DVD release on March 15, 2010. American audiences had to wait a bit longer, with the film becoming available on Video on Demand on April 30, 2010. The terror was then unleashed in high-definition, with the Blu-ray and DVD release on August 24, 2010.

Chapter 18: The Legacy of George A. Romero: Impact on Horror Cinema

In this chapter, we will explore the lasting legacy of George A. Romero and his profound impact on the horror cinema genre. We will examine the influence of Romero's filmmaking techniques, social commentary, and his role in popularizing the zombie genre.

Innovations in Filmmaking Techniques

George A. Romero's innovative approach to filmmaking has had a profound impact on the horror genre. From his early films to his later works, Romero pushed the boundaries of storytelling and visual techniques, leaving an indelible mark on cinema.

One of Romero's most notable contributions was his use of practical effects to create realistic and gruesome depictions of the undead. His emphasis on practical effects over CGI allowed for a more visceral and tangible viewing experience, immersing audiences in the horror of the zombie apocalypse. This approach influenced countless filmmakers who sought to capture the same sense of realism in their own works.

Furthermore, Romero's use of social commentary within the horror genre set him apart from his contemporaries. He used the zombie metaphor to explore societal issues, such as consumerism, racism, and class divides. By infusing his films with deeper meaning, Romero elevated the genre and demonstrated its potential for social critique.

Popularizing the Zombie Genre

While zombies had existed in folklore and cinema prior to Romero's "Night of the Living Dead," it was his film that truly popularized the modern zombie genre as we know it today. Romero's portrayal of the undead as slow-moving, flesh-eating creatures set the standard for zombie lore.

Romero's subsequent films, such as "Dawn of the Dead," "Day of the Dead," and "Land of the Dead," further solidified his status as the master of the zombie genre. Each film expanded on the mythology and societal commentary of the undead, captivating audiences and inspiring a wave of zombie-related media.

Romero's influence on the genre extended beyond his own films. Other filmmakers, such as Danny Boyle with "28 Days Later" and Zack Snyder with his remake of "Dawn of the Dead," drew inspiration from Romero's work, further cementing the zombie genre's popularity in mainstream cinema.

Legacy of Social Commentary

One of the most enduring aspects of George A. Romero's work is his commitment to social commentary. Romero used horror as a vehicle to critique societal issues, exposing the flaws and hypocrisies of contemporary culture. Through his films, he tackled themes such as consumerism, militarization, racism, and the dehumanizing effects of technology.

Romero's social commentary remains relevant today, as his films continue to resonate with audiences. The messages embedded within his work serve as a reminder of the dangers of complacency and the importance of questioning societal norms.

Influence on Future Filmmakers

"Night of the Living Dead" is a true cinematic masterpiece that revolutionized the horror genre and left an indelible mark on the world of filmmaking. Released in 1968 and directed by George Romero, this low-budget black-and-white film not only terrified audiences but also influenced countless filmmakers, shaping the landscape of horror cinema for decades to come. Let's delve into the captivating world of films that were directly influenced by "Night of the Living Dead."

One of the most significant films influenced by Romero's classic is "Dawn of the Dead" (1978), also directed by Romero himself. This sequel expanded on the original film's themes and introduced the concept of zombies roaming a shopping mall. "Dawn of the Dead" not only cemented Romero's status as the master of the zombie genre but also set the stage for the future of zombie films, with its social commentary and visceral scares.

Another notable film influenced by "Night of the Living Dead" is Sam Raimi's "The Evil Dead" (1981). Raimi, a self-proclaimed fan of Romero's work, drew inspiration from the gritty, low-budget style of "Night of the Living Dead" to create his own unique brand of horror. "The Evil Dead" showcased intense, over-the-top gore and a relentless sense of dread, much like Romero's film, and became a cult classic in its own right.

The influence of "Night of the Living Dead" can also be seen in Edgar Wright's comedic zombie flick, "Shaun of the Dead" (2004). Paying homage to Romero's films, Wright infused his own unique blend of humor and horror, creating a genre-bending film that became an instant hit. "Shaun of the Dead" cleverly parodied the zombie genre while still maintaining a deep respect for the films that came before it, including "Night of the Living Dead."

Robert Rodriguez's "Planet Terror" (2007), part of the double feature "Grindhouse," was another film heavily influenced by Romero's work. This gory, action-packed zombie film embraced the grindhouse aesthetic and paid tribute to the exploitation films of the past. "Planet Terror" captured the essence of Romero's original film while injecting it with Rodriguez's signature style and flair.

One film that has been undeniably influenced by "Night of the Living Dead" is Danny Boyle's "28 Days Later" (2002). While not a traditional zombie film, it draws on the concept of an apocalyptic world overrun by infected individuals who exhibit zombie-like behavior. The film's gritty atmosphere, intense pacing, and social commentary owe a debt to Romero's groundbreaking work.

Another film that showcases the influence of "Night of the Living Dead" is Zack Snyder's "Dawn of the Dead" (2004), a remake of Romero's own film. Snyder's version injects a modern sensibility into the story, combining fast-paced action, visceral horror, and social commentary. This remake pays homage to its predecessor while introducing new elements that resonate with contemporary audiences.

Quentin Tarantino's "Pulp Fiction" (1994) may not be a horror film, but it still bears the mark of "Night of the Living Dead" in its non-linear narrative structure. Romero's film challenged traditional storytelling conventions, and Tarantino embraced that spirit by crafting a nonlinear masterpiece that revolutionized independent cinema.

The influence of "Night of the Living Dead" extends beyond the horror genre and into the realm of animation with films like "ParaNorman" (2012). This stop-motion animated film pays tribute to Romero's work by blending horror, comedy, and social commentary in a family-friendly package. It showcases the lasting impact of "Night of the Living Dead" on filmmakers across various mediums.

These films are just a glimpse into the vast array of movies that have been influenced by "Night of the Living Dead." From horror to animation, the legacy of Romero's film lives on, inspiring filmmakers to push boundaries, challenge conventions, and create captivating narratives that continue to captivate audiences to this day.

Romero's legacy also extends to television, with shows like "The Walking Dead" and "Z Nation" drawing inspiration from his zombie mythology. These series carry on Romero's tradition of using the undead as a backdrop for exploring human nature and societal issues.

Romero's Enduring Legacy

George A. Romero's legacy in horror cinema is unparalleled. His innovative filmmaking techniques, social commentary, and popularization of the zombie genre have left an indelible mark on the genre and continue to influence filmmakers today.

Romero's films serve as a testament to the power of horror as a vehicle for social critique and reflection. His work challenges audiences to confront uncomfortable truths and question the world around them.

As we look to the future of horror cinema, George A. Romero's legacy remains a guiding light, reminding us of the potential for the genre to transcend mere scares and entertainment, and offer profound insights into the human condition.

Imagine a warm summer night, where the scent of popcorn lingers in the air and the starry sky sets the stage for an unforgettable adventure. Welcome to the drive-in movie theater, a haven of escapism where families and friends gather in their cars, seeking respite from the monotony of everyday life. As dusk falls, the giant outdoor screen comes to life, casting a mesmerizing glow that beckons audiences into a world of imagination. The drive-in experience was more than just watching a film; it was an immersive journey into another reality, where the boundaries between fiction and reality blurred.

The drive-in movie theater served as the perfect stage for Romero's unique brand of cinematic magic. With its larger-than-life screens and open-air setting, the drive-in elevated the impact of Romero's visually stunning and grotesque imagery. As audiences sat in the comfort of their cars, they were transported into a realm where the undead walked among them, sending shivers down their spines. The collective experience of the drive-in intensified the emotional response, as screams, gasps, and nervous laughter reverberated through the night. Romero's films became a communal journey, connecting drive-in audiences on a profound level and creating lasting memories.

Romero's films left an indelible mark on both the drive-in movie culture and the horror genre as a whole. His visionary storytelling and social commentary paved the way for a new era of horror cinema. The impact of Romero's work can still be felt today, as his influence echoes through contemporary zombie films, television series, and video games. From "The Walking Dead" to "Resident Evil," Romero's legacy lives on, inspiring future generations of filmmakers to explore the depths of human nature and societal issues through the lens of horror.

George Romero's films and the drive-in movie audiences formed a love affair that transcended the boundaries of time. Through his visionary storytelling and thought-provoking narratives, Romero captivated drive-in audiences, transporting them into a realm of cinematic enchantment. The drive-in movie experience provided the perfect backdrop, amplifying the impact of Romero's visually stunning and socially conscious films. Romero's legacy continues to thrive, as his influence permeates the world of horror and ignites the imagination of filmmakers and audiences alike. So, my friend, next time you find yourself at a drive-in movie theater, take a moment to appreciate the enduring connection between George Romero's films and the drive-in movie audiences—a love affair with the undead that will continue to captivate and inspire for generations to come.

Remembering Romero: Tributes and Homages to the Master of Horror

George A. Romero, the master of horror, is renowned for his groundbreaking work in the zombie genre. From his iconic film "Night of the Living Dead" to his "Dead" trilogy and beyond, Romero's contributions to the world of horror cinema are unparalleled. In "Remembering Romero: Tributes and Homages to the Master of Horror," we delve into the life, work, and lasting impact of this visionary filmmaker.

Romero's films not only scared audiences but also challenged societal norms and explored deeper themes. His zombies became metaphors for various social issues, including consumerism, racism, and the breakdown of societal structures. Through his unique storytelling and inventive use of practical effects, Romero revolutionized the horror genre and inspired countless filmmakers.

Let's take a deep dive into some of the notable individuals who have had the privilege of working with him and contributing to his iconic films.

One of the key collaborators of George A. Romero is John Russo. Russo co-wrote the screenplay for Romero's groundbreaking film, "Night of the Living Dead," which revolutionized the zombie genre. Russo's involvement in the creation of the modern zombie archetype alongside Romero solidified his status as an important figure in horror cinema.

Russell Streiner, another significant collaborator, not only worked behind the scenes but also appeared as an actor in "Night of the Living Dead." Born on February 6, 1940, Russell William Streiner is a name that resonates with the film industry. An actor and producer, Streiner's journey in the world of cinema is nothing short of remarkable.

Streiner's voyage into the film industry began with a bang. His role as Johnny in the 1968 classic "Night of the Living Dead" not only marked his acting debut but also his first stint as a producer. This film, a cornerstone in the horror genre, set the stage for Streiner's illustrious career.

Streiner's portfolio as a producer is diverse and impressive. From "There's Always Vanilla" (1971) to "The Booby Hatch" (1976), and the 1990 remake of "Night of the Living Dead", his work spans decades and genres. His cameo as Sheriff McClelland in the remake further showcases his versatility.

Streiner's influence extends beyond the silver screen. His efforts have been instrumental in bringing film and television productions to western Pennsylvania. As the chairman of the board of directors of the Pittsburgh Film Office, his contributions have significantly shaped the region's film industry.

Russell Streiner's cinematic journey is an affirmation to his passion for the craft. His roles as an actor, producer, mentor, and advocate for the film industry have left an indelible mark on cinema. His story continues to inspire the next generation of filmmakers, making him a true icon of the film industry.

Michael Gornick, a talented cinematographer and director, worked closely with Romero on several films, including "Dawn of the Dead" and "Creepshow." Gornick's visual style and expertise in capturing the essence of horror greatly enhanced the impact of Romero's storytelling. Their collaboration resulted in visually stunning and chilling scenes that have become iconic in the horror genre.

Gornick's foray into the world of cinema began humbly, working as a sound technician on George A. Romero's "The Crazies" (1973). His talent quickly shone through, leading to his promotion to cinematographer for Romero's acclaimed film "Martin" (1977).

The collaboration between Gornick and Romero blossomed into a fruitful partnership. Gornick's role as director of photography on films such as "Dawn of the Dead" (1978), "Knightriders" (1981), "Creepshow" (1982), and "Day of the Dead" (1985) showcased his technical prowess and ability to translate Romero's vision onto the screen.

Gornick's talents were not confined to cinematography. He donned the director's hat for "Creepshow II" (1987) and episodes of the TV series "Monsters" (1988) and "Golden Years" (1991). These ventures highlighted his versatility and deep understanding of the horror genre.

Gornick's cinematic contributions extended to the small screen. His directorial work on series like "Monsters" and "Golden Years" demonstrated his adaptability and skill in different formats.

Gornick's passion for cinema extended to teaching and mentoring. He has shared his wealth of knowledge at film events, providing valuable insights into the making of classic horror films.

Gornick's personal life is as intriguing as his career. His stint as a cameraman in the Air Force during the Vietnam War undoubtedly influenced his approach to cinematography and his subsequent work in the film industry.

In conclusion, Michael Gornick's cinematic legacy is a testament to his passion for the craft. His roles as a cinematographer, director, and mentor have left a lasting impact on the world of cinema, particularly within the horror genre. His story continues to inspire the next generation of filmmakers, solidifying his status as a true icon of the film industry.

Tom Savini, a master of special effects makeup, played a pivotal role in bringing Romero's creatures to life. Known for his innovative and realistic prosthetic creations, Savini worked on many of Romero's films, including "Dawn of the Dead," "Day of the Dead," and "Creepshow." His artistry and attention to detail helped establish the gruesome and terrifying visuals that have become synonymous with Romero's films.

Born on November 3, 1946, in Pittsburgh, Pennsylvania, Savini's journey from a young boy fascinated by the magic of film to a revered figure in the film industry is a manifestation of his talent, dedication, and passion for his craft.

The silent-era actor Lon Chaney kindled the spark of fascination in a young Savini. He spent his youth mastering the art of makeup and creating characters that would send shivers down the spine. His relentless pursuit of perfection led him to use "spearmint gum" as a substitute for "spirit gum" in his early attempts at applying prosthetics.

Savini's stint as a combat photographer during the Vietnam War had a profound impact on his work. The gruesome reality of war he witnessed first-hand was later simulated on screen, helping him cope with the horrors of war.

Savini's journey in the film industry began with low-budget horror films such as "Deranged" (1974) and "Martin" (1977). His breakthrough came with George A. Romero's cult zombie film "Dawn of the Dead" (1978), where his ground-breaking special effects took center stage. His work in the controversial slasher film "Friday the 13th" (1980) is often credited with kickstarting the "splatter movie" genre.

Savini's mastery of special effects and makeup is evident in his work on films like "Maniac" (1980), "The Burning" (1981), "Creepshow" (1982), and Romero's third "Dead" film, "Day of the Dead" (1985). His work on "Day of the Dead" won him a Saturn Award.

In 1990, Savini made his film directorial debut with "Night of the Living Dead", a remake of Romero's original 1968 zombie classic. He also directed three episodes of the TV show "Tales from the Darkside" and one segment in "The Theatre Bizarre".

Savini's talent is not just confined to behind the lens. He has showcased his acting skills in films such as "Martin", "Dawn of the Dead", "Knightriders", "From Dusk till Dawn", "Planet Terror", "Machete", "Django Unchained", and "Machete Kills".

Savini's effects work in "Dawn of the Dead" set a high benchmark for zombie makeup. The film was shot in color, unlike its predecessor "Night of the Living Dead", which allowed Savini to indulge in pale undead skin and bursts of crimson blood. His effects were bursting with color, creating a stark contrast to the black-and-white predecessor. Savini's work on "Dawn of the Dead" launched his legendary, long-running career in horror cinema.

Savini's special effects in "Dawn of the Dead" included severed limbs and bite-marks. His work was so authentic and visceral that it defined the zombie genre. His experiences as a combat photographer in Vietnam, where he saw some pretty horrible stuff, influenced his work. He used these experiences to create special effects that looked real because they were based on real-life observations.

In "Creepshow", Savini engineered special effects for each of its five segments. The film thrilled audiences with headless matriarchs, a creature-in-a-crate, a moss man, waterlogged ghouls, and cockroach kills. Savini's work in "Creepshow" is considered his "masterpiece" by many.

Savini's work in "Creepshow" was inspired by his traumatic time serving as a field photographer in Vietnam. He used his childhood passion for creating masks and fake blood to disconnect from the horror he saw and wondered how he could recreate it as a special effect.

In "Day of the Dead", Savini returned to provide the film's special make-up effects. He was assisted by a team of artists that included Greg Nicotero and Howard Berger, who later became known for their work on the television series "The Walking Dead".

Savini's work in "Day of the Dead" continued his tradition of creating visceral and authentic special effects. His experiences in Vietnam continued to influence his work, as he used his knowledge of anatomy and the way blood turns brown as it dries to create effects that looked real.

Savini's special effects work has had a significant impact on the horror genre. His ability to create visceral and authentic special effects, influenced by his experiences in Vietnam, set a high standard for special effects in horror cinema.

John Amplas, an actor and longtime collaborator of Romero, appeared in several of his films, including "Martin" and "Day of the Dead." Amplas brought memorable characters to the screen, showcasing his versatility as an actor. His performances added depth and complexity to Romero's narratives, contributing to the overall impact of the films.

Born on June 23, 1949, in Pittsburgh, Pennsylvania, John Amplas embarked on a cinematic journey that would lead him to become a notable figure in the film industry, particularly through his collaborations with director George A. Romero.

Amplas's breakthrough came with the cult classic 'Martin' (1977), where he portrayed a man convinced of his own vampirism. Originally written for an older actor, the role was reimagined for Amplas after Romero witnessed his performance in a local production of Philemon. This marked the genesis of a prolific partnership between Amplas and Romero.

Amplas's collaboration with Romero extended to films like 'Dawn of the Dead' (1978), 'Knightriders' (1981), 'Creepshow' (1982), and 'Day of the Dead' (1985). In 'Dawn of the Dead', Amplas showcased his versatility by playing multiple roles and serving as the casting director.

Beyond his work with Romero, Amplas delivered compelling performances in 'Toxic Zombies' (1980) and 'Midnight' (1982), directed by John Russo. He also portrayed a weary single blue-collar guy in 'No Pets' and an evil, greedy priest in 'Daddy Cool'.

Amplas's influence extends beyond the silver screen. As a founding member and the Associate Artistic Director of the Pittsburgh Playhouse Repertory Company, and an Associate Professor with the Conservatory of Performing Arts at Point Park University, Amplas has shaped the careers of many aspiring actors.

John Amplas's cinematic journey is an endorsement to his talent, versatility, and dedication. His contributions to the horror genre and beyond have left a lasting legacy, inspiring future generations of actors and filmmakers.

Tom Atkins, a stalwart of the horror and thriller genres, has left an indelible mark on cinema with his performances in films directed by the likes of Shane Black, William Peter Blatty, John Carpenter, Fred Dekker, Richard Donner, Stephen King, and George A. Romero. This chapter focuses on Atkins' unforgettable roles in Romero's films, highlighting his significant contributions to the world of horror.

Atkins' journey with Romero began with the 1982 anthology film "Creepshow". Penned by Stephen King, "Creepshow" is a unique fusion of horror and comedy, presenting five spine-chilling tales inspired by 1950s EC horror comic books. Atkins' performance breathed life into the film, enhancing its overall impact and leaving audiences on the edge of their seats.

In 1990, Atkins and Romero teamed up again for "Two Evil Eyes". Atkins played a homicide detective who finds himself entangled in a web of horror after responding to a 911 call about screaming neighbors. His portrayal of a law enforcement officer added a layer of realism to the film, grounding the supernatural elements in a believable context.

Atkins' roles in Romero's films showcase his versatility as an actor and his ability to bring depth and complexity to his characters. His performances in "Creepshow," "Two Evil Eyes," and "Bruiser" are evidence of his talent and his significant contributions to the horror genre. His collaborations with Romero not only enriched the films they worked on together but also left a lasting impact on horror cinema as a whole.

John S. Harrison Jr., born in 1948, is a multifaceted artist, known for his work as a filmmaker, musician, and composer. His most notable work is his enduring collaboration with the legendary director George A. Romero.

Harrison's journey in the world of Romero began with a minor yet memorable role as the "Screwdriver Zombie" in the cult classic "Dawn of the Dead" (1978). This marked the beginning of his on-screen journey in Romero's universe.

Harrison's involvement deepened with "Creepshow" (1982) and "Day of the Dead" (1985), where he served as the 1st Assistant Director. His talents were not confined to directing; he also composed the haunting scores for both films. His music has since been featured in various other media, including the film "Grindhouse" (2007) and the "South Park" episode "Tegridy Farms Halloween Special" (2019).

Romero and Harrison's collaboration extended beyond films to the small screen with the "Tales from the Darkside" TV show. Harrison wore multiple hats, writing, directing, and composing music for several episodes.

In 2006, Harrison reunited with Romero to produce "Diary of the Dead" (2007). This reunion marked another significant chapter in their collaborative journey.

Harrison's contributions have been pivotal to the success of Romero's films. Their shared journey is a celebration of their passion for filmmaking and their ability to create unforgettable horror classics.

Taso Stavrakis was born on July 12, 1957, in Canton, Ohio. Stavrakis was introduced to Romero through his friend and classmate Tom Savini, a legend in the realm of special effects.

Stavrakis' journey with Romero began with his roles in the films "Dawn of the Dead", "Knightriders", and "Day of the Dead". Romero often humorously suggested that Stavrakis deserved a spot in the Guinness Book of World Records for his numerous zombie portrayals in the Dead series. I can't imagine anyone but Taso in those roles.

However, Stavrakis' contributions extended beyond acting. He showcased his multifaceted talent by assisting with stunts and special makeup effects in several iconic 1980s horror productions. His role as a stunt coordinator in "Day of the Dead" and the Romero-scripted "Creepshow 2" (1987) further solidified his reputation.

Stavrakis' collaboration with Romero has left an indelible mark on the horror genre. His performances and stunt work have become iconic, contributing to the enduring popularity of Romero's films. In a fitting tribute, Stavrakis' brother Christian installed a bronze bust of George Romero in the Monroeville Mall in 2018, the first public monument to Romero's work and career.

Greg Nicotero, a young man from Pittsburgh, was an ardent fan of George Romero's work, particularly the 1968 classic, "Night of the Living Dead". His passion for special effects makeup led him to seek out Romero, a meeting that would mark the beginning of a fruitful collaboration.

Nicotero's first professional involvement with Romero came with the film "Day of the Dead" (1985). Hired as part of the special effects team, Nicotero's work under the tutelage of effects maestro Tom Savini was nothing short of groundbreaking. His innovative makeup and prosthetics brought Romero's ghoulish visions to life, adding a layer of visceral realism that would become a hallmark of Romero's films.

Impressed by Nicotero's talent, Romero continued to involve him in subsequent projects. This consistent collaboration played a significant role in Nicotero co-founding KNB EFX Group, one of Hollywood's leading special effects studios. KNB EFX's work can be seen in many of Romero's later films, including "Land of the Dead" (2005) and "Diary of the Dead" (2007).

The partnership between Nicotero and Romero has left an indelible mark on the horror genre. Their shared vision of graphic, realistic horror pushed the boundaries of what was considered possible in special effects makeup. Today, Nicotero continues to honor Romero's legacy, influencing a new generation of filmmakers with his innovative work. Greg Nicotero's involvement with George Romero's films not only shaped his career but also transformed the landscape of horror cinema.

Nick Tallo, born on April 29, 1947, in Pittsburgh, Pennsylvania, USA, was a widely known actor affectionately popular as Nick "Bomba" Tallo. He was best remembered for his roles in films like "Dawn of the Dead" (1978), "Striking Distance" (1993), and "Inspector Gadget" (1999). He was also the longtime floor manager of the public television show "Mr. Rogers Neighborhood" for over 30 years. However, fans will always remember him as the motorcyclist who rushed into the Monroeville Mall in "Dawn of the Dead".

Nick Tallo passed away on Wednesday, December 14, 2022. He was 75 years old at the time of his passing. The connection between Nick Tallo and George Romero serves as a reminder of the collaborative nature of filmmaking.

It's a testament to the fact that every individual, whether in front of the camera or behind it, plays a crucial role in the creation of cinematic magic. The legacy of Nick Tallo, both in front of the camera and behind the scenes, continues to inspire and influence the world of cinema.

Rudy Ricci, hailing from McKeesport, Pennsylvania, was a man of diverse talents. He honed his skills at the Pittsburgh Playhouse theater school and the University of Pittsburgh. His writing prowess flourished during his university years, earning him recognition from the Atlantic Monthly for his poetry and short stories.

The paths of Ricci and Romero intersected in the early 1960s. Romero, a native of the Bronx, was studying at the Carnegie Institute of Technology (now Carnegie Mellon) when he encountered Ricci. A casual conversation sparked a friendship that would last a lifetime. Romero even resided with Ricci's family in Clairton, Pennsylvania, during his freshman year, and it was Ricci who taught Romero how to drive.

Ricci, Romero, and their mutual friend Russell Streiner founded a company called the Latent Image. Initially focused on creating advertisements, industrial films, and shorts for Pittsburgh public broadcaster WQED's children's series Mister Rogers' Neighborhood, this company would later give birth to the cult classic, "Night of the Living Dead".

The narrative that inspired a multitude of zombie films was conceived and penned in the Green Tree apartment that Ricci shared with his wife. Their apartment became a hub for actor and writer friends, serving as an incubator for ideas.

When it came to casting for "Night of the Living Dead", Ricci was initially envisioned for the lead role of Ben, a resourceful but rough and crude-talking trucker. However, when Duane Jones, a 31-year-old African-American actor, auditioned for the part, his performance was so captivating that everyone, including Ricci, agreed that he should play Ben. This decision was groundbreaking, marking one of the first instances a black actor was cast in a lead role irrespective of his race.

Ricci's contribution to the film industry extended beyond "Night of the Living Dead". He also starred as one of the Motorcycle Gang leaders in George Romero's "Dawn of the Dead" and founded "New American Films", a company that produced numerous local television commercials.

Vincent Survinski, a name born on January 25, 1912, that resonates in the world of cinema, particularly in the realm of horror films. His collaboration with the legendary filmmaker George Romero was not only profound but also instrumental in shaping the landscape of the genre.

Survinski's most significant contribution was to the groundbreaking classic, "Night of the Living Dead" (1968). In this film, he played an uncredited role as Vince, a posse gunman. But his involvement went beyond acting. He also served as the production director, a role that required him to oversee the entire production process, ensuring that all elements of the film came together seamlessly.

During the production of "Night of the Living Dead", Survinski, Romero, and other members of the crew had to stay at the house used in the film. This dedication and commitment to the project were indicative of Survinski's passion for filmmaking and his collaborative spirit.

Survinski's collaboration with Romero extended beyond "Night of the Living Dead". He worked as the Business Manager for "Dawn of the Dead" (1978) and other Romero movies such as "There's Always Vanilla", "The Crazies", "Martin", "Day of the Dead", "Creepshow", and "Knightriders". His role as a business manager involved overseeing the financial aspects of the film production, ensuring that the projects stayed within budget while still achieving their creative vision.

Survinski passed away on May 7, 2001, in Pittsburgh, Pennsylvania, USA. His contributions to the film industry, particularly his collaborations with George Romero, left an indelible mark on the horror genre. His behind-the-scenes work played a crucial role in bringing Romero's visionary ideas to life, contributing to the enduring legacy of these classic films.

In conclusion, Vincent Survinski's connection to filmmaker George Romero was not just as an actor or a crew member, but as a pivotal figure who helped shape the iconic status of Romero's films. His dedication and commitment to his craft serve as an inspiration for future generations of filmmakers.

Regis Survinski, born on December 2, 1928, in Allegheny, Pennsylvania, was a man of many talents.

Regis's entry into the film industry was facilitated by his brother, Vincent Survinski, who was the Production Director on George Romero's "Night of the Living Dead". Regis was brought on board as an investor and, leveraging his background as a firework specialist, he also designed special effects for the film.

Regis's work on "Night of the Living Dead" was instrumental. Alongside his good friend Tony Pantanella, he created the squibs for gunshots, bullet holes, and explosions. They practiced the truck explosion for the film using an abandoned truck at an old mine until they knew exactly what to do. The explosion was done in one take and worked out perfectly.

Regis's work extended beyond "Night of the Living Dead". He worked on other Romero films, including "The Crazies" and "Effects", where he is credited for the special effects. He also had roles in these films.

Regis Survinski passed away on November 2, 2012. His contributions to the film industry, particularly his work with George Romero, have left a lasting legacy. Regis Survinski's work has left an indelible mark on the film industry and serves as a reminder of the unseen heroes behind the scenes who bring a director's vision to life.

Marty Schiff: Imagine starting your film career by fighting off zombies in a mall. That's exactly how Marty Schiff, a theater student from Point Park, embarked on his cinematic journey. His debut was nothing short of extraordinary, as he found himself in the midst of George A. Romero's legendary film, "Dawn of the Dead".

This thrilling start marked the beginning of Schiff's long-standing association with Romero. He went on to feature in several of Romero's masterpieces, including "Knightriders", "Creepshow", and "Deadtime Stories". In "Deadtime Stories", Schiff showcased his versatility by donning the hat of a producer. His collaboration with Romero not only refined his acting prowess but also gave him a unique insight into the world of horror cinema.

Schiff's influence extends beyond his on-screen presence. He has been a driving force in bolstering Pittsburgh's film industry, attributing its growth to Romero's efforts in promoting the city as a filming destination.

Donald Rubinstein: The symphony of horror. Imagine a young artist from Brooklyn, New York, who found his calling in the most unexpected of places - the world of horror cinema. His journey began when he was introduced to the legendary filmmaker George A. Romero by his brother, Richard P. Rubinstein, the producer of Romero's film "Martin".

At the tender age of 26, Rubinstein was entrusted with the task of composing the score for Romero's unique vampire tale, "Martin". Shunning the typical horror tropes, Rubinstein chose to weave a tapestry of melancholic jazz moods, adding a layer of depth and emotion to the film.

The collaboration between Romero and Rubinstein didn't stop at "Martin". Rubinstein went on to compose the score for Romero's Knightriders and the allegorical horror film "Bruiser", and also worked on the main title for the television series "Tales From the Darkside" and its film adaptation. His work extended to the main title and episodic music for the television series "Monsters".

Today, Rubinstein's innovative approach to scoring, which often involves a personal discipline, resonates in the corridors of horror cinema. His compositions, perfectly in sync with Romero's storytelling, have left an indelible mark on the genre. His legacy serves as a beacon for aspiring composers, demonstrating the power of creative risk-taking in the realm of cinema.

Sure, I can help you with that. Here's a compelling 2000-word chapter on the Romero-Rubinstein collaboration:

In horror movie history, few partnerships have left as indelible a mark as the collaboration between Richard P. Rubinstein and George A. Romero. Let's delve into the birth of this partnership, their groundbreaking work in film and television, and the enduring legacy they left behind.

Born in Brooklyn, New York, Richard P. Rubinstein's journey into the world of film and television production began modestly as a production assistant for television commercials. His first significant credit came in the early 1970s as an associate producer for the one-hour TV special "A Night with Nicol Williamson," produced by Dore Schary. However, it was his partnership with horror director George A. Romero that would catapult his career into the limelight.

In the mid-1970s, Rubinstein and Romero co-founded the production company Laurel Entertainment. This marked the beginning of a series of successful collaborations, most notably on the seminal zombie films

"Dawn of the Dead" (1978) and "Day of the Dead" (1985). Through Laurel Entertainment, Rubinstein co-produced or executive produced a number of Romero's films, cementing their partnership as a force to be reckoned with in the horror genre.

Their earliest collaboration was on the film "Martin" (1978), which marked an artistic turning point for Romero. This film was Romero's first feature film collaboration with Rubinstein, cinematographer Michael Gornick, composer Donald Rubinstein, and makeup effects artist Tom Savini. The success of "Martin" laid the groundwork for their future collaborations and set the tone for their unique approach to horror.

"Dawn of the Dead" (1978), another product of the Romero-Rubinstein collaboration, is considered a classic in the zombie horror genre. The film's success led to the creation of "Day of the Dead" (1985), another zombie horror film written and directed by Romero and produced by Rubinstein. These films, with their innovative storytelling and groundbreaking special effects, redefined the zombie horror genre and continue to influence filmmakers today.

The Romero-Rubinstein collaboration wasn't confined to the silver screen. They also made significant contributions to television, producing the 1984–1988 anthology horror television series "Tales from the Darkside". The success of "Creepshow" led to the creation of this series, further expanding their influence in the horror genre.

The collaboration between Romero and Rubinstein has left an indelible mark on the horror genre. Their films, characterized by their innovative storytelling and groundbreaking special effects, continue to influence filmmakers today. Despite Romero's departure from Laurel Entertainment in 1984, the two continued to collaborate, further cementing their legacy in the world of horror.

The Romero-Rubinstein collaboration serves as validation to the power of creative partnerships in shaping the landscape of cinema. Their shared vision and mutual respect for each other's craft resulted in a body of work that continues to resonate with audiences, even decades after their initial release.

These notable individuals, alongside many others, formed a talented and dedicated team that worked closely with George A. Romero to create some of the most influential and beloved horror films of all time. Their collaborative efforts helped shape the genre and solidify Romero's status as a true visionary in the world of cinema.

The Fans

Picture this: a dark room, adorned with posters of the undead, where fans gather to discuss their favorite Romero movies. The air is thick with excitement as they passionately debate the hidden meanings behind every blood-soaked scene. These fans have dissected Romero's films like mad scientists, unraveling the intricate layers of social commentary within.

But it doesn't stop there. These fans go beyond mere analysis and interpretation. They become one with the horror, immersing themselves in the world of Romero's creations. At fan conventions, you'll witness a spectacle like no other. Fans dressed as zombies, survivors, and even Romero himself roam the halls, creating a surreal atmosphere that mirrors the director's twisted imagination.

The devotion of Romero fans knows no bounds. They don't just watch his films; they live them. They construct elaborate sets in their backyards, transforming their homes into post-apocalyptic wastelands. They organize immersive experiences, where participants are thrust into the heart-pounding chaos of a zombie outbreak. These fans are not content with simply being spectators; they want to be part of the horror.

Romero's fans are rebels, challenging societal norms and embracing the darker side of human nature. They revel in the gore, relishing the shock and terror that his movies elicit. For them, Romero's films are a cathartic release, a way to confront their deepest fears and anxieties. They are drawn to the macabre like moths to a flame, embracing the darkness that lurks within us all.

But it's not all blood and guts. Romero fans are also a compassionate and supportive community. They rally together to raise funds for charitable causes, using their love for horror as a force for good. They organize charity screenings, where the screams of terror are transformed into cries of hope and solidarity. Romero's movies may be filled with monsters, but his fans are the true embodiment of humanity.

In conclusion, George Romero movie fans are a breed apart. They are fearless, passionate, and unapologetically devoted. They have embraced the darkness and found solace in the twisted visions of their beloved director. They are the lifeblood of Romero's legacy, keeping the flames of horror burning bright. Join them if you dare, and prepare to be consumed by the unparalleled fervor of Romero's fandom.

The "Living Dead Weekend" is a unique event that takes place in Monroeville and Evans City, Pennsylvania each year. This event was a celebration of the iconic films of George A. Romero, the legendary filmmaker who revolutionized the horror genre with his groundbreaking zombie films.

The "Living Dead Weekend" is a tribute to Romero's legacy, with a particular focus on his "Living Dead" series. The event included movie screenings of Romero's films, thrilling events, and star-studded celebrity appearances. Attendees got the chance to relive the terror and nostalgia of Romero's films in the very locations where they were filmed.

The "Living Dead Weekend" attracted a diverse crowd, from hardcore horror film fans to casual moviegoers. Celebrity guests who had contributed to pop culture, from lead actors to people behind the scenes, were scheduled to appear at the event. However, the event was not just about meeting celebrities. It also included a variety of activities that were both educational and fun.

One of the highlights of the event was the VIP Sunday Brunch at the Cemetery. VIP ticket holders and celebrity guests met at the famous "Night of the Living Dead" Restored Chapel for a catered brunch and greeting session. This was followed by a location tour guided by Lawrence DeVincentz.

Another exciting feature of the event was the "Unseen Night" presentation, where John Soleri and Jim Cirronella revealed rare and never-before-seen images from "Night of the Living Dead". This was followed by a screening of the film.

The "Living Dead Weekend" was more than just a fan convention; it was a celebration of George A. Romero's significant contribution to the film industry and pop culture. By bringing together fans, celebrities, and the community, the event kept Romero's legacy alive and introduced his work to new generations. Whether you were a die-hard Romero fan or just a lover of good cinema, the "Living Dead Weekend" offered an unforgettable experience of terror, nostalgia, and fun.

The Weekend of the Dead event, a unique celebration of Romero's iconic zombie films held in the heart of Manchester, UK. This fan-run event is a two-day extravaganza that brings you face-to-face with your favorite characters from Romero's legendary movies.

From its inception in 2015, the event has grown in popularity, bringing together fans and special guests from around the world. Each year, the event outdoes itself, bringing more and more iconic characters from Romero's classic zombie films to the fans. The 2018 event was a landmark occasion, hosting 13 guests, a first for European fans.

The 2023 event is set to be another blockbuster, featuring, for the first time, a legend from the Walking Dead, Mr. Greg Nicotero. This year, the event will also collaborate with the GARF foundation.

But the Weekend of the Dead is more than just a fan meet-and-greet. It's a deep dive into the world of Romero's classic films like Night of the Living Dead, Dawn of the Dead, Day of the Dead, and the 40th anniversary of Creepshow. The event includes autograph sessions, special prop photo shoots with star guests, and Q&A sessions. Plus, there are stalls selling a wide range of memorabilia, from DVDs and Blu Rays to movie posters, masks, and much more.

The 2023 event will take place at the Inn-side Manchester Hotel, with a packed schedule of guest signings, themed professional photoshoots, guest panels, and vendors. Mark your calendars for Saturday and Sunday, November 4 - 5, 2023.

In conclusion, the Weekend of the Dead offers a unique opportunity for fans of George Romero's movies to interact with their idols and experience a weekend of pure joy. The memories and friendships made at this event are sure to last a lifetime.

The Zombie Walks:

Imagine a sea of people, their faces painted in grotesque detail, their clothes tattered and blood-stained, staggering through the streets in a macabre parade. This is not a scene from a horror movie, but a real-life event known as a zombie walk.

Zombie walks, where participants don the guise of the undead and shuffle through city streets, have taken the world by storm. These events, which began in North America in the early 2000s, have since spread globally, with large cities often playing host.

The first recorded zombie walk took place at the Gen Con gaming convention in Milwaukee in August 2000. It was a tongue-in-cheek response to the Vampire: The Masquerade LARPers who were dominating the convention.

In 2001, Sacramento, California hosted a "Zombie Parade" to promote the Trash Film Orgy's annual midnight film festival. The event, conceived by Bryna Lovig, has since become an annual tradition, attracting over 1,000 participants in 2012.

The record for the largest zombie walk has been broken multiple times. In 2007, over 1,100 zombies descended on Toronto, a number confirmed by the Toronto Police Services. The following year, Brisbane saw an unofficial record of over 1,500 participants.

However, the most impressive record was set in Asbury Park, New Jersey. The Asbury Park Zombie Walk has twice claimed the Guinness World Record for the "Largest gathering of zombies". In 2010, the record was set with 4,093 participants, and in 2013, it was reclaimed with an astonishing 9,592 zombies.

Zombie walks are not just about dressing up and having fun. They can also serve a purpose, such as setting a world record or supporting a charitable cause. Some zombie walks have been organized as "hunger marches" to raise awareness of world hunger and collect items for food banks.

Zombie walks have transformed from a small-scale event to a global phenomenon. They bring communities together, whether for fun, a cause, or to set a new record. These gatherings captivate participants and onlookers alike, proving that even the undead can breathe life into our cities.

The Living Dead Museum, a sanctuary dedicated to zombies in popular culture, boasts a captivating history that reflects the evolution of the zombie genre itself.

Our tale commences in Evans City, recognized as the origin of the contemporary flesh-eating zombie. This charming borough, situated roughly 30 miles north of Pittsburgh, served as the backdrop for the pioneering zombie film, "Night of the Living Dead". In August 2013, the Living Dead Museum first swung open its doors to the public here.

The museum was a key attraction of the Living Dead Weekend, an event that offered a hair-raising experience complete with a plethora of zombie-themed entertainment, film screenings, exhilarating activities, and encounters with celebrities. Fans had the unique opportunity to meet the legends of "Night of the Living Dead" and commemorate this historic event.

However, the museum's tenure in Evans City was temporary. By October 2020, the museum bid farewell to Evans City and unveiled plans to move back to its original home, Monroeville Mall. This relocation marked a homecoming for the museum, which had initially begun as a store and museum named Monroeville Zombies in Monroeville Mall.

Monroeville Mall holds a special place in zombie folklore, as it was the filming site for "Dawn of the Dead", the sequel to "Night of the Living Dead". The museum's relocation to the mall was a fitting homage to the legacy of George Romero, the Pittsburgh director whose films transformed the mall into the birthplace of the modern-day zombie.

Today, the Living Dead Museum serves as a celebration of zombies in pop culture. Nestled in the globally renowned Monroeville Mall, the museum guides fans through a visual journey of zombies in cinema and popular culture. The museum showcases a newly expanded exhibit, divided into themed rooms, where fans can purchase T-shirts and collectibles in the gift shop.

The Living Dead Museum is more than just a museum; it's an expedition through the history of zombies, tracing their roots from Evans City to their present abode in Monroeville Mall. It stands as an establishment to the enduring allure of the zombie genre and a tribute to the imaginative minds that breathed life into these creatures.

So, if you're an aficionado of the undead, don't miss out on a visit to the Living Dead Museum in Monroeville Mall. It promises to be an unforgettable experience.

The George A. Romero Foundation (GARF). This foundation is a tribute to the life, work, and cultural influence of George A. Romero, the "Godfather of Horror".

The GARF is more than just a foundation. It's a commitment to preserving the legacy of George A. Romero and a platform for independent filmmakers and artists who are inspired by Romero's legacy and aspire to continue his tradition of creating quality, socially-conscious horror.

Currently at the helm of the foundation is Suzanne Desrocher-Romero, the founder and president. Alongside her is a team of dedicated individuals including Vice President Tina Romero, Secretary and Treasurer Ramona Streiner, and Chief of Operations Jeff Whitehead. The foundation also boasts a board of members and an advisory board, which includes notable figures in the industry.

The GARF has made significant strides in preserving and promoting Romero's legacy. It has established scholarships and fellowships, undertaken preservation and restoration projects, and awarded the Pioneer Award. The foundation also supports creative projects and has established a Horror Studies Center.

The GARF is a testament to the enduring influence of George A. Romero. It ensures that his legacy continues to inspire and guide future generations of filmmakers and artists. By providing support and resources, the foundation plays a crucial role in nurturing talent and fostering creativity in the realm of socially-conscious horror.

In essence, the George A. Romero Foundation is not just a foundation, but a vital institution that honors the life and work of a legendary filmmaker. It provides invaluable support to emerging artists and filmmakers, ensuring that the spirit of George A. Romero's work continues to thrive in the world of cinema.

The University of Pittsburgh is now home to the George A. Romero Archival Collection, a treasure trove that offers an unparalleled glimpse into the life and work of this filmmaking pioneer. The collection, a compilation of archives from Romero's widow Suzanne Desrocher-Romero, his daughter Tina Romero, and his business partner and friend Peter Grunwald, is a comprehensive portrait of Romero's career. It includes everything from drafts of produced and unproduced screenplays, script notes, budgets, shooting schedules, cast lists, production tests, artwork, correspondence, contracts and agreements, to news clippings, magazines, props, set dressing, promotional materials, posters, and a wealth of audio-visual materials.

The archives offer students, filmmakers, and fans from around the world a unique opportunity to trace Romero's projects from inception to completion. The University Library System aims to establish an international scholarly resource for the research and study of horror and science fiction, building upon existing strengths within Archives & Special Collections. These include full runs of major science fiction pulp titles, thousands of science fiction paperbacks from the 1960s-1980s, an extensive archive of comic books and fanzines, stage performances of horror and science fiction plays, and film scripts from Romero's contemporaries like John Carpenter and Wes Craven, as well as screenplays by authors including Stephen King and Clive Barker.

The George A. Romero Archival Collection stands as an affirmation to Romero's transformative contributions to filmmaking in Pittsburgh, to horror, social, and political cinema, and to the independent film tradition. It serves not just as a beacon illuminating the path of a legend, but also as an inspiration for future generations of filmmakers and fans, daring them to follow in his footsteps.

Staying Scared!

-Brian

Did you love *Staying Scared - The Films of a Horror Movie Legend*?
Then you should read *Creepy Corners in Erie PA*[1] by Brian Dailey!

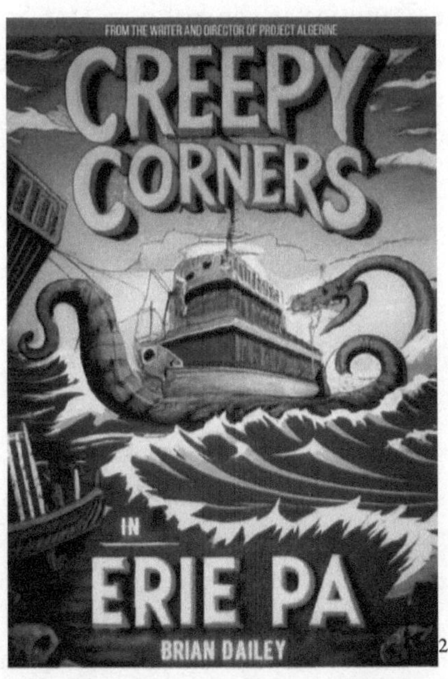

[2]

Erie, Pennsylvania: a city with a rich history and a vibrant culture. It is also a city with a dark side, where strange and unexplained events occur.

In this collection of short stories, you will find tales of haunted roller coasters, mysterious creatures, and government conspiracies. You will also find stories of ordinary people caught up in extraordinary circumstances.

From the bustling streets of downtown Erie to the quiet woods outside of the city, these stories will take you on a journey through the strange and wonderful world of Erie, Pennsylvania.

If you are looking for a thrill ride, this collection of short stories is for you.

---

1. https://books2read.com/u/b5waxR

2. https://books2read.com/u/b5waxR

The Roller Coaster - The 2027 Sigsbee Reservoir Catastrophe - The Fight of Molly Bawn - The Bureau of Scientific Advancement and the Millcreek Mall - The Cottage - The Erie Alien - The Ghost Child of W6th Street - The Zombies at the Soldiers and Sailors Home - The Great Erie Treasure Hunt - The Monster from Lake Erie.

Also by Brian Dailey

The Tavern
Creepy Corners in Erie PA
Staying Scared - The Films of a Horror Movie Legend

www.ingramcontent.com/pod-product-compliance
Lightning Source LLC
Chambersburg PA
CBHW031532150726
47990CB00001B/149